Like Any Normal Day

Like Any
Normal Day

.....

A STORY OF DEVOTION

Mark Kram, Jr.

ST. MARTIN'S PRESS

NEW YORK

www.stmartins.com

Book design by Jennifer Daddio / Bookmark Design & Media Inc.

All photographs are courtesy of the Miley Family Archive unless otherwise noted.

ISBN 978-0-312-65003-2

First Edition: April 2012

10 9 8 7 6 5 4 3 2 1

Contents

Someone to Turn To

Walls of Time

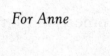

For Anne

What will survive of us is love.

—PHILIP LARKIN

Buddy Miley, six week's before his death.

Jimmy

Strangely, it seemed as if they were up in the air by themselves, suspended in some surreal place beyond words or feeling. Three of them had flown earlier that day to Detroit, and now, going home, it was just Jimmy and Lisa, seated shoulder to shoulder in this cylinder of whooshing sound as Northwest Airlines Flight 1717 carried them back to Philadelphia. As the crew and the passengers stirred inside the cabin, lowering tray tables or unfolding copies of the local papers, the two of them exchanged only a few uneasy glances as if to say, *Did this really just happen?* Lisa held Jimmy by his arm, but could sense that he was scattered in a dozen different places. Jimmy could be like that even on a good day.

Strapped into the narrow airline seat, Jimmy Miley leaned back and caught his breath. In such a hurry to get out of Michigan, he had grabbed his companion, Lisa Lepri, by the hand and butted in line at the reservation counter. Only when their plane had ascended to a cruising altitude did he begin to worry that something could have gone wrong: that Buddy could still be lying there in that hotel room—so cold even with the heat turned up high that his teeth chattered. Standing in the doorway that evening, Jimmy had looked back over his shoulder at his older brother on the bed; not wanting to leave, and yet steered by the urgent command of a voice that hovered nearby: "You better go." So he did, reminding himself, *Do what they tell you. They know. They've done this before.* But as the plane began its approach into Philadelphia International, the vague stirrings of panic that had settled upon him had become unbearable. Nothing had ever gone right for Buddy. Maybe this hadn't either. What if Buddy had changed his mind and he was still in that room by himself, sobbing, "Get me out of here! Where's Jimmy?" As these dire possibilities swirled through his mind, all Jimmy could think was *Man, this sucks.*

On the ground just before 11:00 P.M., Jimmy and Lisa walked quickly through the sparsely occupied terminal and found the van where they had left it in the parking lot close to twelve hours before. It seemed as if days or even weeks had passed since then, that the events that occurred had happened not just in the span of a few hours but in some place far back in his memory. To quell his fevered imagination, Jimmy had told Lisa on the plane that he would call Michigan as soon as they landed, if only to hear someone assure him that his brother was at peace. Climbing up behind the steering wheel of the van, Jimmy searched his overcoat pocket for the contact numbers he'd been given. Scrawled on a piece of paper were two of them. Lisa handed him her cell phone and he began dialing by the light of the dashboard—first one and then the other. "Come on . . . pick up," he said. But it was late and no one did, so Jimmy told himself he would try again in the morning. He would speak with Janet or whoever picked up, hear what he had to hear, and then lie low. Go over to New Jersey and stay with Lisa. He looked over at her in the passenger seat—Lisa, who called herself his "little gypsy girl." She had volunteered to come along to Michigan. Having her with him had been a blessing, yet as he wheeled the van out of the parking lot and eyed the signs for I-95, Jimmy wondered if both of them would end up in handcuffs.

Jimmy remembered what Buddy had told him—Buddy, always calling the plays: "It'll be fine. You'll see."

"Okay," Jimmy said. "Even if it is, what are people going to think?"

"Jimmy? What people? Who?"

"Well . . . you know . . . the neighbors."

"The neighbors? Screw the neighbors."

"And Mom? Did you think of her?"

"That's *all* I've been thinking of."

But Jimmy was still not so sure, even when Buddy said, "Look at me, Jimmy. Mom'll be okay." In the array of appalling outcomes that played inside his head, Jimmy suspected that she would be far from okay, that she would slam the door in his face and never let him back in the house for taking her boy away. No one would have blamed her—including Jimmy. But when Jimmy called ahead from Michigan to his sister Linda and told her what had happened, she had told him adamantly, "Get the hell out of there, Jimmy. Come home! Right now!" Uncertain, Jimmy paused and said, "Can I? Are you sure?" Linda told him, "We're all here waiting for you." And they were. When he parked the van back at the house, his older brother Bob came out and gave him a hug. Inside, everyone else embraced him, too—his four sisters, his father, Bert, and even his mother. Whatever tears Rosemarie Miley would shed would be done in the privacy of her bedroom—later—in keeping with the stoicism that had been handed down to her by her Irish ancestors. No one would shun Jimmy the way he had feared—in fact, just the opposite would be true—yet he would always sense that something hung in the air between them: this "thing." To give air to the grief that had taken root inside him, he would bring it up in conversation, only to have the room grow uneasy and someone change the subject. Uncharacteristically, Rosemarie once even snapped at him, "That's just something you'll have to live with." Jimmy just shrugged: No one would ever want to hear the details.

Acorn Drive was asleep under the glow of a March moon as Lisa got into her car and headed back to New Jersey. Bob took Jimmy home with him to keep an eye on him. Jimmy looked pale, the energy gone from his six-foot-two, 220-pound frame. For a period the two brothers sat up and talked—Bob asking the questions, Jimmy beginning to droop with exhaustion. "Everybody still loves you, you know that," Bob told him. With the pillow, sheets, and blanket Bob then provided, Jimmy curled up on the couch. Odds and ends from the day passed before his eyes: how they told Mom they would be going to the eye doctor; how Jimmy had helped Buddy from his wheelchair onto the bed at the hotel; and how it had seemed to take forever before there came that tap on the door. Jimmy opened it and in walked Dr. Death—Jack Kevorkian—who had disappeared with his grim equipment into the bathroom. Lisa sat on the edge of the bed and looked at Buddy.

"So is this still something you want to do?" she said. "You can change your mind at any time."

"Yes," Buddy said.

"Well, then I have one favor to ask of you: Send me white feathers. I love you, Buddy."

That it would be Jimmy who ended up taking Buddy to Kevorkian came as a surprise only to those who did not know how attached the two of them were. When word began circulating of what had happened, some would say in disbelief, "Jimmy did what? Jimmy?" But Buddy understood that he could count on Jimmy, who had once flown with him to France to seek healing at the Sanctuary of Our

Lady of Lourdes. Others had helped Buddy in large and small ways for years, but when it came to this . . . his death . . . there was no one else he could ask to help him who would set aside their apprehensions and say yes. While Jimmy would not for a second yield in his belief that he had only behaved as any loving brother should, he would discover that this act of devotion would leave him as paralyzed in his own way as Buddy, who as a high school quarterback, twenty-three and a half years before, had sustained a spinal-cord injury and had been left a quadriplegic. Jimmy would come to think of himself as the arms and legs Buddy could no longer use.

Buddy: What a fine athlete he had been. Everyone who saw him play had said so. Only seventeen years old, good-looking, and talented in football, basketball, and baseball, he carried himself with a swagger that would leave opponents spoiling to separate him from his teeth. "He had life by the ass," says boyhood friend Guy Driesbach. Girls swooned over him, the way he evinced such a sincere interest in them—and that long hair! Coaches were somewhat less enamored with his flashy style, his oppositional attitude—and that long hair! But even they had to concede that he could have gone far were it not for that fall day in 1973 when, in just a few seconds, life suddenly had *him* by the ass and irrevocably altered the destiny of not just himself but countless others. Steeped in the lengthening shadows of the ordeal that consumed Buddy, whole lives were swept up and dropped in different places by what happened, as if a big wind had come along and left behind downed wires that would spark and flare for years after his death.

Sleepily, Jimmy rolled off the couch, not sure for a second or two where he was or if what had happened the day before had been some weird hallucination. Bob was still asleep in his bedroom. Jimmy padded to the bathroom, where he surveyed himself in the mirror. Gone was the chiseled face of the young baseball star he had once been. But his blond hair was still the same as he always wore it—shaggy in the back and on the sides—and he still had long-ball power in his arms, only now he used it to "haul shit" from place to place in the moving van he had saved up to buy. He splashed some cold water on his face, slipped into his overcoat, and headed back home, thinking that he should stop somewhere along the way to pick up milk and the papers. But he told himself he would do that later, once he had had a chance to call Michigan. At 7:00 A.M., he stood in his living room and again dialed the number he had for Janet Good, who had assisted Kevorkian the evening before. Jimmy gazed out the window at his overgrown backyard, where an old heavy bag hung from a tree limb.

Someone picked up.

"Is this Janet?" Jimmy asked.

"Yes."

"This is Jim Miley. Um, I was calling to see, you know, if it worked?"

"Buddy is at peace, Jim. It took seven minutes."

"That fast?"

"I held his hand and he talked about you and your mom. We said an Our Father. And he closed his eyes."

Jimmy paused. "So, now what . . . what should I do? Go someplace? You know, leave town?"

The woman simply told him, "Just act as if this were like any normal day."

Trajectories

. . . . .

Bert Miley and Rosemarie Quinn, 1944.

ONE

. . . . .

Prayers Before Sleep

Nothing thrilled her quite so thoroughly as stepping onto the dance floor. As a young woman of sixteen, Rosemarie Quinn would take the subway each Friday evening to the Benedict Club in Philadelphia, a home away from home for servicemen who were stateside during World War II. In the four-story building at Fifteenth and Race Streets, dedicated formally just three days after the Japanese bombed Pearl Harbor, soldiers and sailors would stop by to eat, shoot pool, or enjoy the companionship of a local girl before shipping out overseas. Mind you (as Rosemarie would always add in years to come, in case anyone would get the wrong impression), it was all good, clean fun. Under the aegis of the Archdiocese of Philadelphia in conjunction with the USO, the club forbade the young ladies who served as hostesses to wear sweaters or saddle shoes, the former too sexually suggestive for the setting and the latter not dressy enough.

In an old photograph that Rosemarie would keep from one of the formals, you can see her in the center of the crowded dance floor, her face full of gaiety and unacquainted with worry. Junior hostesses had to be eighteen or older, but Rosemarie changed the year of her birth on her baptismal certificate from 1925 to 1923, not an unconscionable deception given the war effort and the cute fellows who poured into the place. On Friday evenings she would approach one—or he would introduce himself to her—and they would sway under the elegant baritone of Bing Crosby as his song "The Very Thought of You" played on the jukebox. *The mere idea of you, the longing here for you.* She loved Glenn Miller and His Orchestra, too—his song "In the Mood," especially—which would bring the room alive with jitterbugging couples. But even under the surveillance of the senior hostesses, older women assigned to assure that the young ladies switched partners with regularity and that there was no untoward behavior, it was not uncommon for passions to bloom and nuptials to ensue.

So young and unworldly, Rosemarie became atwitter with a few crushes of her own and even won a few proposals, albeit none that propriety would ever allow her to divulge once she became spoken for herself. But when she was still single and looked upon the opposite sex with an appraising eye, she would arrange to join them on the corner when the dance ended (strictly against the rules!) and slip off with them and a group of her friends for a slice of pie at the popular automat Horn & Hardart. The boys would even accompany her back home to Broad and Erie on the subway and sit with her over a cup of coffee until her 1:00 A.M. curfew. When they would ship out to Europe or the Pacific, Rosemarie would send letters overseas to them with news of the home front, storing away whatever reply she received in a drawer by her bed. Only years later would she wonder what destiny had held for them, if the prayers she said before sleep had been answered and the young faces who had beamed at her across the dance floor had indeed grown creased with age. It saddened her to think that so many of them had surely died in battle.

Going to the Benedict Club on those evenings would leave Rosemarie in giddy anticipation. Friendships formed with girls from across Philadelphia that would endure for years, and there were always encounters with French or English servicemen, who were stationed at the Navy Yard while their ships were being repaired. Some would become sweet on her, engaged by the twinkle of innocence in her eyes, yet they would be off again in two weeks or so, gone again to a war that seemed so far away from the tranquil universe she inhabited on Carlisle Street. There, the cheerful young Rosemarie occupied a three-bedroom house with her parents, James and Rose, and her four siblings: Jim, Bob, Jack, and Frankie, a Down syndrome baby who had been handed over to Rose at the hospital by an unsympathetic nurse who told her, "Take the idiot home." Given that these were the Depression years, the house became a sanctuary for the odd uncle or aunt who was out of work. Rosemarie says, "My father was the type who would give up his bed to somebody if they showed up at his door. He was just that way."

Pop had come to America in his early twenties from Cookstown in county Tyrone just before World War I. Unable to find a job in Ireland, he landed work at the Philadelphia Navy Yard and became acquainted with Rose at a dance. With a dense Irish brogue, he carried himself with a certain reserve, which he used to his advantage when he found a job in the 1920s as a waiter at the stylish Bellevue-Stratford Hotel. There, he befriended the wealthy Philadelphians of the era, including the heirs to Keystone Saw Works founder Henry Disston (whose son Hamilton became one of the early developers of Florida). Family legend is that James received stock tips from the Disstons and others and that he lost a significant sum when Wall Street crashed in the fall of 1929. No one would ever be sure how much—Pop would never say, and no one ever asked him. But even so he was always employed, and the weight of the Great

Depression did not fall as cruelly upon the Quinns as others, albeit Rosemarie remembers slipping cardboard into her shoes and that Pop always gave the boys haircuts. "Oh," says Rosemarie, "how they used to scream!"

Crucifixes and renderings of the Blessed Mother peered down from the walls of the house. The Quinns were devout Catholics and observed the Church calendar accordingly: 10:00 A.M. mass on Sundays; novenas on Monday evenings; and confession on Saturdays, where it is likely Rosemarie found herself assessed an Act of Contrition for that illicit editing of her baptismal certificate. A "good girl" by the standards of the Church and in the eyes of her parents, Rosemarie was just an average student at Little Flower Catholic High School. She'd had hopes of studying to become a nurse one day, but was stymied by the chemistry course that was part of the curriculum. So when she graduated on June 6, 1942, she got a job as a secretary for the *Philadelphia Record* and that same year moved on in the same position to Exide Battery at Nineteenth and Allegheny, where she handled the paperwork in the personnel department. Too young at that point to even think of settling down, she imagined only in passing the man she would one day marry: Whomever she gave her heart to would have to be a Catholic and a good dancer.

Albert Miley was neither. To begin with, he was a Protestant, which immediately placed an obstacle before her. Moreover, he was an awkward, unenthusiastic dancer, despite having been a fine high school athlete in the Philadelphia area. But when Rosemarie found herself working with him at the employment office at Exide, she encouraged the interest he seemed to take in her. "He had on saddle shoes," Rosemarie says. "That seemed funny for working in an office." Rosemarie remembers she asked a friend, "How do you kiss a guy with glasses?" The friend giggled and replied, "Very carefully."

On their first date, they went to see a Red Skelton sidesplitter that was playing downtown and Bert laughed so hysterically that Rosemarie turned her head: *My gosh!* When Bert was drafted soon thereafter, they spent the evening before he reported at a dance at Sunnybrook Ballroom in Pottstown. "Glenn Miller and His Orchestra played," says Rosemarie. Bert told her, "When I get back, I am going to marry you."

Letters between the two crisscrossed the ocean, yet Rosemarie was still so young and . . . uncertain. "I was going to be darn sure before I told somebody I loved him," Rosemarie says. Just before the war ended in September 1945, she even considered joining the Marines; she had gotten to know some women who were in the Corps at the Benedict Club. But Bert had discouraged that. With the world at peace again and impending prosperity in the air, he came home, settled back into his job at Exide, and followed through with his plans to propose. Rosemarie said yes. But both sets of parents had some concerns regarding the mixed marriage. The Quinns liked Bert well enough, but Rose told her daughter, "It's going to be a little difficult." Neither Rosemarie nor Bert had any intention of asking the other to convert, yet Rosemarie did insist that he present her with her engagement ring before a statue of the Blessed Mother at St. Stephen's Church. Catholic canon prohibited the couple from exchanging vows in a church, so they did so on February 1, 1947, in the rectory there and set out that Saturday evening for their honeymoon in Manhattan. There, they stayed at the Taft Hotel and saw young comedian Jackie Gleason perform his act at the Diamond Horseshoe. At another stop they squeezed their faces into a cardboard cutout of an island couple under the words HEAVEN CAN WAIT—THIS IS PARADISE.

But Rosemarie found that the carefree days of just a few years before were gone. Marriage changed her life in ways that she had not expected, especially given the diagnosis Bert had received a few years before in the air force when he contracted a case of the mumps. A doctor told him he would be unable to have children. "Ha," Rosemarie says with a wry laugh, "I would love to get my hands on that doctor today!" She became pregnant with Bob in 1948 and found herself housebound while Bert got up and went to work. Starved for news of the outside world, even if it was only for a shred of gossip, she grew annoyed with how incommunicative Bert had become, the way he would sit at the table and eat his dinner encapsulated in long silences. One day in 1950 she came to her breaking point. Bert had left for work that day and had said or done something. Incensed, Rosemarie, strapped one-year-old Bob in his stroller and began walking from their one-bedroom apartment in Germantown until she came to her old house on Carlisle Street over an hour later. Inside, her mother looked at her with surprise.

"What are you doing here?"

"I left Bert."

Rose Quinn sighed. "Come on and have some lunch. Your brother Bob will drive you back home."

When Bert came home that evening, he didn't know she had left . . . and life went on. Six children followed Bob: So their lives went on uninterrupted. By the time Bert arrived back at the apartment that evening, Rosemarie had settled down and did not tell him where she had gone or what she intended. In the ensuing years, six more children followed Bob: Joanne (1951), Rosemarie (1953), Buddy (1956), Patti (1958), Linda (1960), and Jimmy (1961). In search of an outlet away from Bert and the children—along with a way to bring in some money, which had become increasingly tight—Rosemarie found a part-time job in 1963 as an aide on the labor and delivery floor at Holy Redeemer Hospital in Abington. While she worked the

11:00 P.M. to 7:00 A.M. shift on Fridays and Saturdays and got only a few hours of sleep on the weekends, she enjoyed getting to know the other nurses and occasionally having lunch with them. But what she could not have known is that the job was also preparing her for an event nine years later that would call on every ounce of her resolve.

Bert at Warrington Athletic Association.

TWO

Boyhood Fields

I t was hard ever to know what Bert was thinking. From the day
he began working at Exide Battery in 1941 until he retired forty-
three years later—other than the three years he served in the air
force in World War II—each day was a replay of the day before and
the day before that. In a pressed business suit, clean white shirt, and
plain tie, he would report each morning at Exide at 8:00 A.M., clock
eight hours as a personnel manager, and appear in his driveway back
home at 6:00 P.M. with the punctuality of the tides. Though he would
never be an avid churchgoer, he would always think of himself as a
"good-living person," a by-the-book Republican who voted the party
line because his parents had done so before him. But when it came to
talking politics or world events or even what happened that day at
work, Bert evinced no interest in even a passing conversation.
Within his household he would come to be viewed by some as aloof,
yet a part of him softened in the presence of his daughters.

"No look-see," he would remind them as he changed into his lei-
sure attire in his bedroom at the end of the day.

Giggling, the children would turn away until he was done dressing.

"Okay," he would then say. "Look-see!"

Even as he ate dinner, he had one foot out the door to Barness Field, where he coached football in autumn and baseball through the spring and summer at the Warrington Athletic Association. Bob and then Buddy and Jimmy played for him. In these twilight hours each day he seemed to fall in stride with the man he longed to be, a person whose authority was unquestioned and whose presence commanded attention. "It became an integral part of his life," says Bob. Bert even had a hand in building the dugouts at the field, where he always seemed to have winning teams. But while he had a keen eye for the finer points of play, whatever praise he doled out to his players would be followed by a *but* and some small correction. "Good going on that double play but . . . ," he would shout out at his shortstop and second baseman, yet never with even a trace of profanity. Stationed behind the counter at the snack stand on game days, Rosemarie watched her seven children grow up at Barness Field: As the three boys moved up in age groups, the four girls paraded up and down the sidelines with pom-poms.

With blond hair and blue eyes, Bert had been an exceptionally fine athlete during his youth, better in football than in baseball. The son of a milkman and former textile-mill worker who weathered the Great Depression better than others in his family—an unemployed uncle was forced to sell apples on the corner to scrape together a few dollars—the six-foot, 160-pound Bert excelled as an end in football at Germantown High School, where as a junior and senior in 1939 and 1940 he was selected to the All-Public League team. In an era during which the protective equipment consisted of leather helmets without face guards and a scarcely adequate layer of padding beneath the uniform, Bert found himself in a pickup one day when he carried the ball on an end around and "went down and stayed down." Dazed, he wobbled off the field but was fine. "It could have been a concussion," Bert says. He also had a propensity for bloody noses, usually the consequence of an elbow thrown by an opponent at the bottom of a pileup. "Football is football," Bert says with a shrug. "It is a game of hit and be hit."

Even then football held a claim on something deep within young men such as Bert. Symbolically, as an adult he would look upon it as a bridge that ushered boys into manhood, a teaching vehicle that endowed them with an understanding of competitiveness, teamwork, and resiliency. He would have agreed with the observation of General Douglas MacArthur, who once said the game endeavored "to build courage when courage seems to die, to restore faith when there seems to be little cause for faith, to create hope as hope becomes forlorn." Whatever truth was in that grandiose assertion, it was also true that the sport has forever embraced a level of barbarism that once alarmed even "the Rough Rider" himself, President Theodore Roosevelt, a football advocate who in 1905 called for sweeping reforms to curb an escalating death toll. While the sport would never be entirely free of peril, the dangers that remained embedded in it called upon young men to prove themselves in ways that no other sport could ask of them. In the crucible of action that unfolded on the fields of his boyhood, Bert learned life lessons that he would carry into old age. And it was perhaps one of the few periods that he could look back on and say that he ever truly had fun.

Bert admits he would have liked to go to college. But his grades were just average and that held him back from a chance at playing at the University of Delaware, where a coach recommended that he attend a year of prep school. Instead, he played sandlot ball, found that job in the employment office at Exide, and in the fall of 1942 began dating Rosemarie. Within a few weeks, he heard from his draft board and was off to serve. Waving good-bye from the platform to his parents, Albert and Florence, and his sister Florence—Rosemarie did not join them, saying now "it was an occasion for family"—he boarded a special train for new inductees in Philadelphia and headed off to New Cumberland, Pennsylvania, where he was issued his GI gear and began a hitch that eventually deployed him to Tinian Island as the radio operator of the B-29 bomber. From the bomb-bay window of the Lady Jane, he saw the war unfold in a way that seemed surreal to him, far removed from the bloodletting that ensnared the troops below in the hot sands of the Pacific theater. While he says he never reached his breaking point in battle, he would remember a mission one hellish night over Japan.

"We dropped our bombs over some city and these huge fires flared up," Bert says. "I remember thinking they reminded me of the Sunoco refineries in South Philadelphia, how they used to catch fire and shoot flames into the sky. Well, we got caught up in the lights, and the Japs began shooting their ack-ack at us. I could hear it exploding outside our ship. And there was a Jap Zero shooting at us from behind. We got out of the lights and got caught up in a violent updraft, which lasted thirty seconds or more. We went up eighteen hundred feet just like that. The way we were being tossed around, I was just hoping the wings would stay on the damn airplane. We finally got out of that when suddenly the bombardier, who was in the nose of the ship, shouted, 'Pull up, Red! Pull up, Red! Pull up, Red!' We almost hit another B-29."

Bert shakes his head as he remembers seeing that city on fire and says, "There was no way in hell anyone could have lived through that inferno."

Whatever impression that apocalyptic scene left on him, it became just another thing Bert kept locked inside himself. But as Rosemarie later concluded, that was just the way men were when they came back from the war, less inclined to discuss the particulars of combat than to just get on with life. Within hours of stepping off the train back in Philadelphia in December 1945, Bert got out of his uniform, donned his civvies, and—as Rosemarie says with a laugh—sent her a telegram that asked, "Can we go out on a date Saturday night?" Bert had announced his ardent intentions toward her in his letters, of which Rosemarie received four or five each week, and before long he was on bended knee. To celebrate their engagement, the couple boarded a bus to the Pocono Mountains, only to discover a problem with their reservation upon their arrival at their hotel. Only one room had been set aside for them instead of the two that had been requested. Sweetly Rosemarie says, "So we got back on the bus and came home. Good girls know where to draw the line!" Grimly Bert adds, "I remember."

Housing was scarce in Philadelphia due to the reentry of the servicemen into the community. But in the early days of their marriage, the Mileys found an apartment on the third floor of a house in Germantown. Under the impression that he was incapable of fathering children, Bert had not even considered the possibility of parenthood until Rosemarie announced that she was pregnant. It surprised yet tickled him: A boy—if it was a boy—would allow him an opportunity to indulge his passion for sports, perhaps even to add an ending to his own unfinished story as an athlete. Given the handicap that her brother Frankie had come into the world with, Rosemarie was just relieved that Bob was healthy when they placed him in her arms in March 1949. Secretly, she had hoped for a girl and two years later got her wish when Joanne was born. Bert says, "I said, 'Well, fine, that's a nice family. Let's stop here'. That didn't happen." Overhearing that, Rosemarie observes, "Well, he had something to do with it!" But the increasing pressure of keeping up on a small income would get to Bert. In a reflective mood he admits, "I just wish I could have given the kids more."

Material things?

"Yeah," he says. "Material things."

Larger quarters had to be found with the arrival of Joanne, so the Mileys purchased a three-bedroom house in the Mount Airy section of Philadelphia that had gladiolas planted at the base of a white picket fence. Child number three—young Rosemarie, later called Mimi—was born there in 1953. But within a few years the white exodus to the suburbs was in full swing, and Bert and Rosemarie found a three-bedroom rancher on a three-quarter-acre lot for $14,000 in Warminster, then a community of wide-open fields that had come into the hands of developers. As the moving truck backed up to the house with their belongings in September 1955, Rosemarie was showing with their fourth child.

Albert George Miley, Jr., was born the following January. Concerned she would not be able to get to the delivery room in time from so far out in the country, Rosemarie stayed overnight in the city with her parents and, on the day that labor would be induced, took a subway by herself to the University of Pennsylvania Hospital. In the bundle the nurses later handed her was an eight-pound, twelve-ounce boy that Rosemarie remembered as being "perfect—a really good-looking baby." Though she thought it was a good idea to name the boy after his father—which would be something of an irony, given the friction that would develop between the two in the years to come—Rosemarie was not sold on calling him Bert or even Al. Her sister-in-law Florence came up with an alternative. Off the top of her head, Aunt Floss said, "Call him Buddy." Bert looked down at the baby in his crib and placed a football next to him.

. . . . .

Buddy at age three.

THREE

Where All the Nuts Lived

Whenever it happened, you'd hear the cry of sirens; not one, but dozens of them calling across Bucks and Montgomery Counties. Perhaps you'd even see a plume of black smoke billow up somewhere off on the horizon. Either way, you'd know another plane from the Willow Grove Naval Air Station had fallen out of the sky. Manning the base on Saturdays and Sundays were Naval and Marine Air Reserve pilots—or weekend warriors, as they were informally known—who would take jet fighters up for training exercises that did not always end in safe landings on the yawning, eight-thousand-foot runway. Such tragic occurrences became a point of some contention in the early 1960s, when an FJ-4 Fury plowed into the Green Hills Day Camp at the edge of the base during a summer picnic. Eight people died and another fifteen were injured. Some area homeowners voiced fears for their safety, and some even called for the closure of the base, but they were shouted down in public hearings by their neighbors, who stood up and proclaimed, "Where would you have them go, Moscow?" and "Do you want a red star flying over your head?"

Jets passing overhead became such a part of daily life that you just stopped hearing them. Given her eternal appreciation for men in uniform, Rosemarie did not join in the campaign to close down the base. "They were here before us," she says. But when aviation pioneer Harold F. Pitcairn sold the airfield to the navy in 1942 in support of the war effort, the site was still surrounded by undeveloped acreage that bore some resemblance to the New Jersey Pinelands. Not until the war ended did the area become increasingly populated—and thus an issue for stalled aircraft—as pillbox houses sprang up alongside the few farms that one by one would vanish in years to come. Sue Schultz moved onto Acorn Drive just before the Mileys did and remembers how it was not uncommon during the dinner hour for a pig to wander away from a trough and waddle down the street. From the cockpit of the jets that buzzed by in the early 1960s—occasionally including the Blue Angels, which came in so low that Bob remembers, "You could look up and see the face of the pilot seated at the controls"—the topography that slipped by below became dotted each year with more rooftops.

Rosemarie became fond of saying, "Acorn Drive: the place where all the nuts lived!" With the arrival of Patti in 1958, Linda in 1960, and finally Jimmy in 1961—by which point Rosemarie looked heavenward and implored, "O Lord, not another one!"—the Miley family grew to seven children as the baby-boom generation unfurled across America. Up and down Acorn Drive and the surrounding streets, every household seemed to be overflowing with children: Sue and George Schultz had seven children, the Bushmans had six, the Ratcliffs ten (or was it twelve?—no one could remember). On summer evenings, adults sat outside on their porches as the air sang with the cheerful commotion of boys and girls who played leapfrog, ate snow cones, and chased fireflies with jars. The boys played baseball up at the Ratcliff place with a ball held together with electrical tape and a cracked bat secured by small nails. Sue Schultz remembers how her daughter Diane and the younger Miley girls would stop traffic as they strolled down the center of the street twirling batons. "There were oodles and oodles of kids," Sue says. "They moved from backyard to backyard. Oh, it was wonderful."

The Miley house was always a hub of activity. In the big field that adjoined it, where a game always seemed to be in progress, Bert hung an old tire from a tree limb that the children would climb on and swing from; Buddy used it years later to sharpen his accuracy by throwing footballs through it. The house was a three-bedroom rancher with a partially finished basement. When everyone was still home, the four girls shared one of the bedrooms and the boys the other. They slept in steel bunk beds acquired from the navy base. When Bob headed off to Millersville State College in 1967, Buddy moved down into the privacy of the basement, where he installed a chin-up bar at the foot of the stairs. Jimmy soon followed him down there. Buddy claimed the lower bunk, Jimmy occupied the upper. Buddy would come in late on a Saturday as a teenager with his friend Guy Driesbach in tow and, as Jimmy feigned sleep, spend hours going over the events of the evening. Jimmy would hear Buddy laugh and ask, "Guy, did you see how hot that girl was?" Or he would say, "I laughed my ass off when he did that." Jimmy would bury his head beneath his pillow and giggle.

Generally, the brothers got along well: Bob looked after Buddy, and both looked after Jimmy (sort of). Bob stood as godfather for Buddy and later spent hours with him playing catch, leaning back and launching pop-ups high in the air for Buddy to circle under and snap at with his glove. When Bob had a paper route as a twelve-year-old, he delivered the *Evening Bulletin* on his bicycle with Buddy perched on the center bar. Buddy would hop off in front of a house, grab a paper, and run it to the porch. There, he would open the door and toss it into the living room. No one locked his door in Warminster back then. One year when Bob was at Millersville, he invited Buddy and his friend Billy Gallen to come out and stay with him for a week to sample a slice of college life. Bob came home one evening and found them sitting at a table with a roommate playing poker, each of them with a can of beer and a cigarette. And as for the always-annoying Jimmy, Bob once poured a shot of whiskey in a glass of milk just to see if it would calm him down. On another occasion, Bob and a few of his siblings grabbed Jimmy, buttoned him up in a coat with a hanger in it, and hung him up in the hall closet. Jimmy says with a laugh, "I was abused as a boy."

With a face full of freckles and an unruly mop of dirty-blond hair, Jimmy had been a challenge from the day he was born. Rolling her eyes in exasperation, Rosemarie says, "I knew he would be a handful when he came out and peed on the doctor." Jimmy would do the same as a boy of nine or so, when, in a prank that would be typical of his silliness, he sat up in a tree and urinated on the head of Donnie Schultz, whose sister Diane retaliated by winging Jimmy in the forehead with a rock. Neither Donnie nor Diane remember that incident, but Diane says that it could certainly have happened, given the code of honor in the neighborhood: "If someone picked on your brother, you stuck up for him." Jimmy remembers that Bert ushered Diane into the house and forced her to apologize to him. But Jimmy and Donnie would play ball and periodically end up in what Donnie characterized as "knock-down, drag-out fistfights." Donnie says, "He clocked me every time."

Jimmy was always getting into one thing or another. *Goofy* is the word that always comes up when his old friends think back on him. Driesbach remembers that when you spoke to him, Jimmy tilted his head at you "sort of like a Labrador retriever." Told again and again not to play in the creek that curled along the edge of the property, where he and his friends used to dive with bare hands for minnows, Jimmy so exasperated Bert with his habit of strolling through the door with wet sneakers that Bert commanded him to sit at the dining-room table holding them up to dry. "I sat there for an hour," Jimmy says. "Seemed liked four." Through his early school years, he was a disinterested student, earning only average grades as his attention wandered to playing sports. At the Warrington Athletic Association, he followed in the footsteps of Bob and Buddy, a more accomplished athlete than either of them, even if years later that would become a point of contention to Buddy. When Bob once told Buddy that Jimmy was the better athlete, Buddy shot back, "You've got to be kidding!"

Buddy and Jimmy: How inseparable they would become. Jimmy looked up to him, just as Buddy had looked up to Bob. Yet Jimmy was afraid of Buddy, too—understandably. "Oh, boy, Buddy had a temper," Jimmy says. While Buddy was always protective of him, especially when he came to steering Jimmy away from dope users ("Smell that?" Buddy would say as he sniffed the air. "Weed. Stay away from that"), he also used his five-year age advantage to push Jimmy around. He would shove a big drum case at him and say, "Here, carry this to school for me." And Jimmy did, up a steep incline of what seemed to be an unending sidewalk, his hands unable to get a solid grip on the unwieldy instrument. By then a talented youth-league pitcher, Buddy would take Jimmy into the backyard and throw to him. Without any equipment, Jimmy crouched down with his glove up and his knees closed tight as Buddy reared back and peppered him with fastballs, one after another as Jimmy stabbed at the white blur that came hissing at him. Occasionally, the ball would skip up, strike him in the shin, and send Jimmy running into the house in tears.

"Mom!" Jimmy would howl as he slammed the door behind him.

Buddy would throw his glove at him, follow him inside, and yell, "Come back here, you big baby! Be a man!"

Whatever quarrels erupted soon passed, and they would be back outside in one improvised game or another. One was called wire ball, which utilized a tennis ball and the apron of utility wires overhead in the street. One player would toss the ball up in the air and try to hit one of the wires on the way down, each of which had a designated value: One would be a single, another a double, and so on. "But it would be an out if the other player caught the ball," Jimmy says. On other occasions they played a form of handball in the schoolyard with a group of six or so neighborhood friends. One would throw a tennis ball against a wall, and each player would have to volley the ball back with his palm. Whenever a player messed up, he was assessed a point. Anyone who collected three points would have to stand against the wall as the others had a turn at hurling the ball at his backside.

And what did they call that game?

Jimmy laughs and says, "Ass ball."

Only echoes of those summer evenings would remain in the years that followed, of voices up and down the street calling out as twilight fell, "George, come home!" "David, come home!" The games would break up and one by one the boys would head home, some running but others just leisurely twirling their gloves in the air. Mosquitoes would drive the adults from their lawn chairs and back inside, where they would sit with the paper as a Phillies game purred on a transistor radio: "And here comes the two-two pitch to Johnny Callison . . ." At the Miley house, the windows would be left up, and by dawn a cool breeze would be flowing in, and on it the far-off sound of the bugler at the navy base playing reveille.

. . . . .

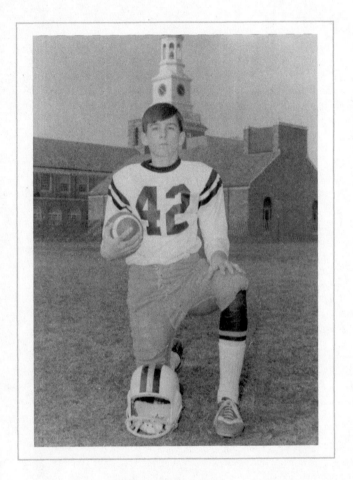

Buddy with the Little Quakers.

FOUR

Head-to-Head

On a summer evening when they were thirteen or so, Buddy and Guy Driesbach crawled under the fence at the Bucks County Drive-In Theater and immediately encountered a pair of feet. Upon looking up, they saw that the feet belonged to the theater manager, who told them to stand up and come along with him. As they walked, Driesbach explained that they were there to join their parents, who were out there somewhere in the tangle of cars jammed in the parking lot. The manager eyed the boys skeptically but said okay, he would page them at intermission. "But they better be here," he said. "Or I'm calling the police."

Driesbach leaned over to Buddy and whispered, "On three, we're running."

Buddy nodded.

Driesbach began counting, "One . . . two . . ."

But before he came to *three,* Driesbach turned and bolted out the back gate and toward a nearby cornfield.

Someone shouted, "There he goes!"

Just as quickly, Buddy took off, too, catching up with Driesbach as the two veered into the high rows of horse corn. Their pursuers—the supervisor and another employee—soon gave up. But the boys continued crashing through the corn, the ground beneath them soggy from a thunderstorm that had passed through. Buddy lost one of his sneakers and said, "I gotta go back." But Driesbach looked over his shoulder at him and said, "Bud, I'm runnin'." Rosemarie remembers how her shoeless son showed up with his friend in her living room: "Oh, they gave me some cock-and-bull story about what happened."

Driesbach joined Buddy the following day in the cornfield in his search for the shoe. "It was tough to find," Driesbach says. "We had to do some sneaking around because the owner of the place, Joe Penrose, was a no-nonsense old farmer. But we eventually found it where he left it. In the mud."

Going back as far as anyone can remember, Buddy seemed to be always in motion, if not in flight from teenage high jinks, then on some athletic field in pursuit of what people agreed had been his animating goal: to one day flee Warminster. It was not just that the crowded house he grew up in had become too confining (which it had), or that he and his father were always at odds (which they were). In the way that the young often do, he looked upon the world his father occupied as too small for the dreams that he harbored. Other than the years he spent in the air force, the only place Bert had gone to was to work, the Warrington A.A., and back home again. But Buddy had larger plans, beginning with a college, preferably somewhere far away—Arizona State perhaps. One day he planned to coach, too, settle down with a wife and children, but not before he was thirty and had had a chance to get his fill of life. Depending upon how things worked out, he could even see himself playing some pro ball.

Early photographs of him as a lanky youth show him in Clark Kent glasses and a Beatles mop top. But even then he was ahead of the boys his age when it came to athletics. When Buddy was seven or so, Rosemarie overheard a parent say of Buddy, "That kid is too good. He has to be older than they say." But it was not just his skills that set him apart, the speed and agility he had as a quarterback or the live arm he had as a pitcher. In whatever sport he played he exuded an aggressiveness that seemed to spring from some anger deep inside him. One could see it in how he would drag a pile of tacklers for a few extra yards, and how he would buzz a batter under the chin just to keep him from taking a toehold at the plate. Given the way he played, it was not uncommon to see him up on crutches or with his arm in a sling.

Only the elite young football players in the Philadelphia area were chosen for the Little Quakers, an all-star team founded and coached by Bob Levy, who would become better known as the owner of the Belmont Stakes winner Bet Twice. Some two-hundred boys would try out each year for forty spots on the team, which in 1969 had a five-game schedule that included trips to play teams in New Orleans and Hawaii. Levy anchored his philosophy in two areas—blocking and tackling—and worked the players hard during the selection process because, as he says, "we had to see who could play." In keeping with the hard-nosed ethic of the era, during which head-to-head contact was looked upon as a way to prepare players for contact and not as something that could be harmful to them, the Little Quakers performed drills that would years later be frowned upon by orthopedic experts. Levy says that back then no one knew any better, but adds, "Kids can get hurt doing anything." As for the relative safety of football, Levy would always say of his players, "You can't put 'em in a glass case."

One of the drills the Little Quakers frequently used was "the nutcracker," whereby two players lay on their backs head-to-head, ten yards apart. One of them had the ball. At the sound of the whistle, the players scrambled to their feet and rammed into each other—generally, with their heads—as the ballcarrier tried to get by the defender. Pat Delaney, who played on the Little Quakers in 1969 with Buddy, says that he once shattered his helmet participating in the drill; years later he still had the pieces. Vividly, he remembers the day Buddy faced off with a running back who, Delaney says, was "a big, big guy." Their two helmets collided in what Delaney says was a "violent hit . . . you could hear it across the field. And you knew Buddy was hurt." Buddy, who had an especially long neck, complained of stiffness that was later checked out by a doctor. Asked if he was in any pain, Buddy said no, fearing that he would be told to wear a neck brace. He had seen a classmate wear one and worried that it would detract from his appearance.

"Does it hurt?" the doctor asked.

"Nothing hurts," Buddy said.

The doctor pressed, "Are you sure?"

Buddy assured him he was fine.

Buddy would later regret that answer, yet that was Buddy—always so vain. While Buddy did not play again that year, he stayed with the Little Quakers. Initially, Delaney thought of him as "a pain in the ass." Buddy was a cutup, given to snipping the shoelaces of his teammates before practice. "So you would be late getting out to the field and have to run laps," says Delaney, a squat strong safety who remembers telling a teammate of Buddy's, "I'm gonna crack this kid." That year the Little Quakers went to Hawaii to play the Marine All-Stars, the sons of servicemen stationed in Pearl Harbor. Someone in authority had the idea to house the two teams in the same barracks, which Delaney remembers led to a brawl that had the MPs out in full force. Levy then moved the team to a posh beachfront hotel, where Buddy thought it would be hysterically funny if he ordered room service for six rooms. "Pancakes, eggs, sausages, were being brought up, enough to feed an army on what just came to each room," says Delaney. "The coaches were furious, asking everyone, 'Who did this?' And there was Buddy standing off to the side, saying, 'How did this happen?'"

Coaches found Buddy to be a challenge. Whatever ability he had was offset by his being headstrong. In an era when old-school coaches were still coming to terms with the emergence of flashy, look-at-me-style players, Buddy worshipped at the altar of Joe Namath, the New York Jets quarterback who favored long hair and white cleats, and "Pistol" Pete Maravich, the dazzling LSU and later NBA player who enchanted crowds with his floppy socks and behind-the-back, look-the-other-way passes. At Archbishop Wood High School, Buddy pitched for the varsity as a freshman and aspired to play quarterback. Bert remembered how his son once substituted himself into a freshman football game for a defensive play. "And he did it without telling the coach!" Bert says. "That was what I objected to." But that was just the beginning of his problems at Wood, where the varsity football head coach demanded that his players get buzz cuts. "I asked one of the assistant coaches one time, 'What happened to Buddy at Wood?'" says Brian Sheehan, a classmate there with Buddy. "The coach told me, 'Buddy would not get a haircut.'" But Sheehan remembers that was just Buddy, who had some of the same goofball in him that Jimmy did.

"I remember how he used to go into an ice-cream place across from Archbishop Wood," says Sheehan. "He would stand at the counter, order an ice-cream cone, and—and I saw him do this—he would smash it into his forehead."

Seeing that he had no chance of playing quarterback at Archbishop Wood, Buddy transferred to William Tennent, where the head coach, Bill Juzwiak, had heard that Buddy was "hard to handle." But Juzwiak would discover just the opposite was true, that Buddy was attentive, dedicated, and hardworking. Given his ambitions to play in college, Buddy knew that he would need to have an excellent senior year to attract some interest from colleges. "When I got him, he was highly motivated," says Juzwiak, who saw in Buddy not just ability but a willingness to give of himself to his teammates. "What I used to try to get across to the players is this: 'We are here to accomplish something together. And whatever else you do, you have to keep playing hard. Keep playing hard and eventually the other guy will quit.'" Juzwiak says, "Buddy was never any kind of problem. He just wanted to play."

In a fundamental way, Buddy was just like Bert, even if neither of them admitted it or even recognized it. Both were oppositional when it came to hearing the opinions of others. Bob says of his father, "Whenever you would say, 'Yes,' he would say, 'No.' Challenge him and he would just get louder . . . and then shut down altogether." Some of that same obstinacy could be found in Buddy, who Bob says had trouble dealing with authority figures other than Juzwiak. Delaney says, "If the world went right, Buddy went left. And then he would try to talk you into why you should go left." In some ways Buddy and Bert were like hissing fuses at opposite ends of the same stick of dynamite: One or both were bound to blow.

"The old man was tough as nails," says Billy Gallen. "He was always screaming and yelling at Buddy."

Over what?

Gallen chuckles. "Just regular shit."

How Buddy wore his hair and otherwise carried himself on the field ate at Bert, who was old-school himself when it came to how a player looked and behaved. From his conservative perspective, the boy was the epitome of a hot dog, which is to say "someone always calling attention to himself." Communication between the two was always lacking. Bert remembers he told Buddy when he was fourteen that he should work to physically strengthen his apparently fragile neck, but that Buddy "probably said nothing." Whenever he had to dole out some critique, Bert says he passed it along to Rosemarie instead of addressing it to Buddy himself. Jimmy remembers a day Bert stood by the dugout at an American Legion game Buddy pitched.

"Come on, follow through!" Bert yelled.

Buddy looked over at him and shouted, "Get out of here! Go home!"

Gallen says, "I think I remember that happening on a couple of occasions."

But Buddy was nothing if not cocky, the quintessential alpha male. Guy Driesbach remembers an American Legion game Buddy pitched during which Driesbach committed two consecutive errors at shortstop. Buddy called him over and scolded, "You've got to start catching the ball!" Sure enough, Driesbach booted yet another one, and Buddy walked off the field, shouted to some girls who were watching, and got into his car with them. When his astonished head coach, Joe Bocklet, asked him where he was going, Buddy replied, "The pool. If he can't catch the ball, I'm outta here." Bocklet benched them on another occasion, which led to the friends going AWOL. "Next thing you know, we were in a car with a girl Buddy had started talking with in the stands," Driesbach says. "She drove us over to her house, where we ate peanut-butter-and-jelly sandwiches. Buddy loved peanut-butter-and-jelly sandwiches. By the time we got back to the field, Joe had never known we were gone."

Girls were enamored with Buddy, just the way they were back then with his idol, Joe Willie Namath. But it was not just his appearance they found so attractive: the six feet one, 175 pounds set off by a head of hair that protruded from the back of his cap. Driesbach remembered that Buddy had "a good rap" to go with his athletic build. "He was the big man on campus," says Betsy McAfee (formerly

Sheehan), who attended grade school and later Wood with Buddy. But not until a few years later would Buddy become acquainted with a young woman who would settle into a place in his heart, someone who would peel back the layers of boyhood and give him a glimpse of the man he would long to be.

. . . . .

Karen Shields at William Tennent High School.

FIVE

. . . . .

Karen, Are You Here?

S he remembers the station wagon driving off, the gravel churning under the wheels as her older sister waved good-bye to her
through the rear window. It had been a day full of laughter and
games, a navy picnic an hour or so away from her home in San
Diego, and now suddenly seven-year-old Karen Shields found herself running for the car and shouting, "Wait for me!" She stopped
and stood there, certain they would turn around and pick her up. But
the car just drove on, and she was left alone. A woman who found her
told her that she was a friend of her parents' and sat with her at a picnic
table, where Karen folded her hands in her lap and looked down at
her clothes, the white blouse and yellow shorts now soiled from a day
of play. Quietly, her brown eyes began to fill with tears.

"It's okay," the woman told her. "They'll be back."

Cars left the parking lot one by one as the two sat there. It was
getting dark by then, and it seemed to Karen that a long time had
passed. Gently, the woman told her that she could come home with
her and that they would stop for ice cream on the way. But just as

they were preparing to leave, the station wagon pulled up and her parents, Bob and Janet, got out. As they spoke with the woman and her husband, Karen climbed into the back of the car, where her sister laughed and told her, "No one knew you weren't with us until we were almost home." Bob slid back behind the wheel, looked back over his shoulder, and began counting heads. From that point forward, he would always do that and ask before he drove away, "Karen, are you here?"

Given how shy she was in her early youth, it was easy enough to lose track of her, particularly in that big, often loud household. As the third of six children, she would come to think of herself as a classic middle child, too young to play with her older siblings and too old to play with her younger ones. Her sister Linda would describe her as "invisible," a characterization that Karen herself would only partially buy into. From her perspective, she was more or less a typical navy brat: always on the go. By her teenage years, she had come to understand that no place was more than temporary, and that friendships tended to evaporate as soon as her parents again weighed anchor. "Children of career military parents have no continuity to life," says her younger brother, Tom. "Everything gets severed. You get close to people and you have to break it off. So you just have to keep re-creating yourself over and over."

But if Karen went unnoticed occasionally, she herself seemed to notice everything. Whenever a move was forthcoming, she would immediately know because less and less food would be in the refrigerator. It was jarring and would, years later, account for the way she would keep her own refrigerator overstocked to provide her with a sense of permanence. As Bob Shields worked hard during his twenty-three-year career in the navy to give his high school sweetheart and their children a better life than he had experienced as an impoverished boy in New Hampshire, Karen crisscrossed the country during her early childhood with stops in Tennessee, Indiana, Florida, California, and New Hampshire. In the picturesque house Bob had found for them in Keene, New Hampshire, which contained hidden passages that had been used to hide slaves during the Civil War and sat atop a rise surrounded by springs and brooks, Karen would lie in bed upstairs and listen as her mother sat at the kitchen table each evening and wrote letters to Bob in Vietnam. "The way the vent system was in the house, I could actually hear her pen on paper," Karen says. "It was almost like a lullaby."

Inevitably, it was always an adjustment when Bob came back from overseas. The loose rein that Janet held on the children was pulled tighter, and the independence that the children enjoyed diminished. "Whenever we knew Dad was coming home, tension would settle into the house," says Tom, who was a year and a half younger than Karen. But some of it was simply that he had been gone for so long. At the dinner hour, as the Vietnam War escalated, Karen would watch Walter Cronkite each evening on an old black-and-white TV that had a crack across the screen. Still a young child then, she searched the fuzzy picture for her father in the scary footage from Southeast Asia, thinking that if she could somehow see him in the background for only one second, she would be able to sleep easier. When he rotated stateside, she was excited to see him again; yet a part of her was afraid of him, too; she had become accustomed to the soothing manner of her mother and would cower whenever he lost his temper. Clumsy, she always seemed to have scraped knees or stubbed toes, which prompted her mother to say more than once, "Karen, you could trip over the pattern in the rug." Karen remembers how she used to spill her milk at the dinner table, not once or twice but so frequently that she urgently reminded herself before she sat down:

Don't spill the milk.

Don't spill the milk.

Don't spill the milk.

And she would always spill it. Always.

"Dammit, Karen!" Bob would shout.

Janet would eye him sharply and say, "Bobby, hush!" With a towel, she would wipe it up as if nothing had happened.

Health problems plagued Karen even then. Off and on during her early childhood, she would run high fevers that no one could seem to get to the bottom of; her mother gave her ice baths to lower her temperature. But it was an incident on the day the family was scheduled to move from New Hampshire to Warminster in 1971 that would leave an enduring impression on her. At a campground just outside Keene, Bob looked over at Linda and Karen and said, "One of you go gather up some firewood, and the other go inside the camper for the pizza." As the two girls raced inside for the pizza— the easier job—Linda pushed Karen from behind, which sent her accidentally over the edge of a cliff. At the bottom of the ten-foot drop, she landed face-first on a brick wall and shattered her jaw in four places. She remained behind at a hospital in Keene for two weeks and later required additional care at the Philadelphia Naval Hospital, where in the wards she encountered the staggering toll of Vietnam.

In a chilling yet somehow noble spectacle up and down the hospital corridors, she came upon men without arms and legs and even faces. Some of them were scarcely older than she was. One of the places critically injured soldiers were sent once they were stabilized enough to be flown by air back to the United States, the Philadelphia Naval Hospital provided Karen with exposure to a hidden aspect of the war seen not even by her father, who had performed his duty thirty or so miles offshore on aircraft carriers. Wide-awake as she had her jaw realigned, set, and rewired, a procedure that was done without anesthesia due to a shortage of it, Karen remembers that the doctor told her before he rebroke it that it would be over before she knew it, and that if she wanted to cry, she should just "look around at some of the soldiers in this place." She did. In the three weeks or so that passed, during which she played pool, checkers, and chess with them, she came to understand the brotherhood that existed between the men, how even the angriest of them would help each other in and out of artificial limbs, and how some of them just wanted to get well enough to rejoin their buddies "in country." Girlfriends and even wives had left some of them or soon would once they became acquainted with how combat had disfigured them.

By then no longer a child but a blossoming young woman, Karen enjoyed the old clapboard farmhouse the family settled into in Warminster. Surrounded by land—sixty-four acres—it had nine bedrooms, one of which she shared with Linda. While Karen could be somewhat solitary, given to spending hours alone in her bedroom writing in her journal, she became more animated when she attached herself to a cause, some activity that seemed to call her to a larger purpose. Contrary to the conservative political leanings of her parents, she came to think of herself as a free spirit and dressed accordingly in peace signs, huarache sandals, and hip-hugger jeans. She attended sit-ins, fielded calls for a suicide hotline, and, in her junior year at William Tennent High School, volunteered one day a week at a state mental institution, the exposure to which would take her days to shake off. Socially, she dated occasionally, but an attempted sexual assault the summer before her senior year left her traumatized. While swimming laps one evening at the pool where she worked as a lifeguard, a male coworker several years older dived in and pulled her under. She slipped from his grasp and hiked herself out of the pool, but the attack continued. The man forced himself on top of her, pressing down until it became difficult for her to breathe. But again she squirmed free and he finally gave up. As he walked off, he looked over his shoulder, laughed, and told her, "Grow up." For Karen, the ordeal would occupy a place of shame and be something she would never speak of.

So, the first day of school of their senior year, she eyed Buddy Miley with understandable standoffishness. Surrounded by his new teammates and some cheerleaders, he sat on a table during an assembly in the cafeteria, a pair of crutches at his side due to a foot sprain suffered during a preseason game. Because she had no interest in football, she had never seen or even heard of him. As Coach Juzwiak spoke of the season ahead and introduced Buddy, whose presence would, the coach seemed certain, assure a winning year, Karen allowed her gaze to linger on the six-foot-one quarterback with long hair that fell just below his collar. Karen remembers thinking how he exuded a relaxed air. When Buddy later stood to leave, he looked over at her and paused, as if he had come upon something unexpected. Neither of them knew what to do, or say, so they just laughed, said, "Hello," and went off to their classes.

Some connection had occurred between them. Karen was certain of that. It left her feeling giddy—and apprehensive. When they were in class together, she would catch Buddy looking at her, even giving her a silly wink. She would immediately blush. *Damn*, she would think. *What is it about this guy?* The question would play in her imagination, but she never had an answer for it. Whatever had occurred was full of energy, albeit the two of them were as opposite as two people could be: the jock and the hippie chick. Ordinarily, Karen favored the company of artists, bookish types, not someone who could throw a football sixty yards. But soon the glances and winks led to playful conversations between classes—and an occasional touch. While they had still not met outside of school by the end of September, Buddy asked for her phone number and promised to call after the Plymouth Whitemarsh game that Saturday. He told her, "We can go somewhere and talk." When the call never came, Karen just shrugged and thought, *Maybe something came up.*

Buddy, star quarterback.

SIX

O Dear Lord

Quarterbacks aggravated Carmen Frangiosa, Jr. It was nothing personal, just that quarterbacks carried themselves with an air of superiority. To begin with, you could never get near them during practice. They would wear a sleeveless top over their jersey to set them apart from their offensive teammates, and they always seemed to have an assistant coach nearby to stand guard over them, just in case Frangiosa or one of his defensive teammates charged through the line and got too close. He remembers that if you even brushed up against the quarterback in practice, the coaches would chew your ass out. Game day could not come soon enough for him each week.

On the Tuesday before the William Tennent game, Plymouth Whitemarsh coach Ed Charters summoned his star middle linebacker to his office and gave him his assignment for that Saturday: Get a helmet on Buddy Miley. Given to operatic displays of temperament, Charters patterned himself in style after legendary Alabama coach Bear Bryant, even down to the houndstooth hat that sat perched on his bald head. Charters had assembled one of the better high school teams in Pennsylvania in 1973, a commonly held assertion that even Penn State coach Joe Paterno endorsed in a congratulatory letter he sent to the team at the end of the season. But Charters had seen some film on Buddy and knew that he could create problems, particularly with his running ability. The five-foot-eleven, 220-pound Frangiosa understood precisely what Charters wanted him to do to Buddy if he took off running: Make him pay the price.

Collegiality between rivals had no place in the Suburban One Conference back in the 1970s. "It was year-round, pure hatred," says Frangiosa, who would years later scratch his head whenever his son would shake hands with an opponent upon leaving the field and say, "See you at the party!" No one extended a hand to an opponent back when Frangiosa played, unless it was attached to a forearm to the chin. Although he knew Buddy from playing baseball against him, Frangiosa looked upon him as just another obstacle in a sport where the coaches had always told him he was too small. The son of a World War II veteran who had seen action in the Battle of the Bulge, Frangiosa remembered that Charters and others played on that insecurity, even when he won *Parade* All-American honors that senior year and Notre Dame and some forty other colleges came to recruit him. Frangiosa says, "I definitely had a chip on my shoulder."

Scattered clouds hung over southeastern Pennsylvania that Saturday, the ground wet from some showers that had passed through the area. Early that morning, Buddy bounded up from his bedroom in the basement and found his sister Rose sitting on the living-room sofa. Wearing his helmet, Buddy jogged back and forth across the carpet and asked her, "How does my hair look?" It spilled from beneath his headgear and swished this way and that. "It looks good, Bud," his sister told him with a giggle. Cousin Bobby Miley, Jr. (or Bobby J), drove over to William Tennent with Bert and Buddy and remembers that Buddy was "in a good mood, eager to play that day." In the locker room, Buddy stripped out of his street clothes, got his foot taped for extra support, and slipped into his uniform, yanking his jersey down over his head and tying a towel to his waist. Giving special attention to his cleats, he wrapped them in white adhesive tape, bestowing upon them the razzle-dazzle of the shoes Joe Namath wore with the New York Jets. With his helmet and shoulder pads under his arm, he then boarded the bus with his teammates for P-W.

Only Bert and Bob had come to see Buddy play that day. Rosemarie had been overcome by an "odd feeling" and instead accompanied Jimmy to his game at the Warrington A.A. As the P-W players stretched on the opposite side of the field, Buddy walked up to the fifty-yard line, pointed at them, and said, "All you guys are overrated. We'll see what happens after today!" Frangiosa says Charters would have "crucified us" if he or any of his teammates had engaged in such theatrics, so he just looked over at fellow cocaptain Steve Nauta and said, "Are you watching this guy?" As Buddy yakked, Frangiosa could feel the fury build up in himself, thinking, *YOU are doing THIS on OUR field?* But not until the game began did he and Buddy exchange words.

As Buddy crouched behind center, Frangiosa glared into his eyes. "You've got a big mouth, huh?"

"Yeah," Buddy said. "And I can back it up."

On the sideline that day with a broken leg, P-W offensive tackle Steve Bernardo remembers that both teams that day played "physical, physical football." Although Tennent was 0–2 and overmatched in every aspect of the game, they played with uncharacteristic abandon behind Buddy, who undressed the swarming P-W defense with his running ability. "Buddy was a wiseass, but the better he did against us, the better he got," says Bernardo. P-W safety Mike Dippolito remembers Buddy "chewed us up" with his agility and speed, and that he was "taking big chunks of yardage." When he connected with end Craig White on an eleven-yard touchdown pass in the first quarter, Buddy jumped up and called to his opponents, "What about that! What about that! What about that!" Frangiosa passed Buddy as he was leaving the field and told him, "You throw one touchdown pass. What do you want—a medal?" But Buddy just grinned at him. Frangiosa remembers, "He was enjoying it, really in the moment. He was playing well and he knew it."

But Frangiosa was livid. "So pissed off I could have killed him," he says. P-W defensive coordinator Reese Whitely summoned Frangiosa and assigned him to shadow Buddy. "Whenever he goes, you go," said Whitely, once a star quarterback at the University of Virginia. "We have to get on this guy. I want him hit every time he touches the ball!" But Frangiosa would hit him "whether he had the ball or not," which began to unnerve Buddy, who looked up at Frangiosa and asked, "What are you doing?" Frangiosa sneered at him and replied, "Take a look at me. Get used to it." At the end of a passing play, Frangiosa rammed him with a shoulder, tripped over him, and gave him "a little shot on the way."

"How do you feel now?" Frangiosa asked. "Gonna do that cheer-leading thing again?"

Bodies flew across the line of scrimmage with increasing intensity on each play. As P-W continued to apply pressure on him, Buddy grew irritable and began upbraiding his offensive linemen. Frangiosa chuckled and said, "What are you yelling at them for? Aren't you the superstar? You've got the shoes for it." But the rangy quarterback just laughed as if to say, *Bring it on.* "Real hard hitting," says Frangiosa, who also played guard. On a P-W offensive play in the second quarter, he inadvertently plowed down his own fullback, Tim Erlacher, from behind. Erlacher writhed on the ground in howling pain. Ordinarily, Erlacher would have tried to find a way to get up and walk off the field on his own power to spare himself the wrath of Charters for using up a time-out. But he looked down at his shattered ankle and waved to the coaches for help. As Erlacher sat on the sideline in an air cast, P-W scored, went ahead 7–6 on the extra point, and kicked off.

Calling out the signals as the P-W defense edged in closer to the line, Buddy leaned over center at the Tennent forty-yard line and called out an option play. Buddy could have looked downfield for one of his receivers, handed off to running back Mark Dougherty, or kept it himself and run. In the split second he had to decide, Buddy spotted a hole open up off left tackle and charged into it. From his safety position, Dippolito chose not to drop back into coverage but to stop any possible run. Buddy dodged him, but Dippolito remembers he clutched a handful of his jersey as Buddy sped by. Six or seven yards upfield, P-W defensive tackle Grant Hudson caught him by the foot. But it was Frangiosa who had an angle on him. With an eight-to-ten-yard running start, he plowed into him at chest level with the rage that had been building in him since Charters had handed him the game plan. Buddy flipped over and landed on his neck. Under a pile of squirming bodies, Buddy emitted an anguished squeal.

"*Eeeooowww!*"

Then . . . "I'm gonna die. I'm gonna die."

No one who was close to him would ever forget the noise that came out of Buddy. Some would go on to play in college and even the pros, where they would become intimately acquainted with the sound track of injury—the crunching of helmets, followed by the guttural cry of a player who had shattered a knee or an arm. But this was somehow worse, hard for any of them to describe except to say, as Hudson would, "You immediately knew that this was something bad." Hudson was overcome with a sick feeling, accompanied by the sense that the day had suddenly become surreal. Ordinarily, Buddy would have bounced back up with a grin, if only to show his opponent that he had the biggest balls on the field. But he just remained there on the ground, facedown, as Tennent running back Bob McCarney stood over him.

"Yo, Bud," his old friend said. "Come on, man. Get up."

Frangiosa waved to the Tennent sideline and urged, "Somebody get out here! Quick!"

Suddenly, worried onlookers converged. Up among the increasingly uneasy spectators, Bert left his seat and headed for the field, his face fixed in a deep frown as he waded through the crowd. Bob, in his first year as a history teacher at Tennent, was seated elsewhere with a colleague, Bob Kennedy, and waited for a sign of some movement. When there did not appear to be any, he told Kennedy, "I think he is paralyzed." Urgently, he hopped a fence and walked over to the crowd that had formed around his brother. Juzwiak was kneeling down by then to attend to Buddy and remembers thinking, "This cannot be happening. Good God!" Frangiosa just looked on in horror until one of the coaches approached him with expelling hands and asked him and his teammates to stand back. Frangiosa says that he is 100 percent sure that Buddy had movement in his upper body.

What happened at that point is a blur, stored by some in an unreachable place in the unconscious mind. But clearly no one immediately knew what was wrong with Buddy, only that he was incoherent, in shock, and something had to be done. Because of the way he had fallen, and the angle that his head was in, some conjectured that he had shattered his collarbone. Some suspected his arm had been injured, perhaps even his leg. Frangiosa remembers as he looked on in deepening panic that Charters scolded him, "He has a broken arm! What the hell is your problem?" Frangiosa replied, "No, this guy is bad, Coach." But while P-W had a doctor on the sideline who came out to attend to Buddy, Frangiosa remembers, "No one took control of the situation," in part because of the wild screams that welled up from the fallen player. No one suspected a spinal-cord injury, which can be the only explanation for why such standard precautions as sliding a board under him and stabilizing his head were not observed. Someone rolled Buddy over on his back. Someone else undid his chin strap and removed his helmet. McCarney and some other players lifted him up and placed him on the stretcher that had been provided by the attendants of the ambulance that had parked by the field. His eyes glazed over with confusion, Buddy looked at McCarney as they moved him and, as his head jiggled to one side, grunted, *"Ugggghhh!"*

McCarney says, "I swear that was when he crushed his spinal cord."

With Buddy strapped on the stretcher, the crew maneuvered him into the rear of the ambulance and began to close the door. "Get his legs in!" shouted Bert, who had jumped up into the back of the vehicle. On the way from the field, the ambulance stopped off at the P-W sideline to pick up Erlacher, who was placed on the bed across from Buddy. Erlacher says the driver called ahead to Sacred Heart Hospital in Norristown and said, "We have two football players, both with a possible broken leg. Bringing them in." Erlacher remembers thinking, *My leg is not possibly broken. My leg is broken.* Upon hearing what the driver had said—that Buddy had a possible broken leg—Bert said sharply, "He is hurt worse than that!"

With its siren howling, the ambulance sped away as Bert sat in the back and stared at Buddy, not knowing what to say as this boy who had so challenged him whimpered, "O dear Lord, thank you for seventeen years of life. O dear Lord, thank you for seventeen years of life. O dear Lord . . ." On and on he uttered those words, as

Erlacher exchanged glances with the attendant stationed in the rear and thought, *I've got a broken leg and I'm not hamming it up like that.* But years later Buddy would remember he told himself over and over, as he lay there enveloped in shadows, *Keep your eyes open.* Because he was sure if he allowed them to close, he would never open them again.

A Window
on
Acorn Drive

.....

QB Is Paralyzed In Tennent Game

By JIM GAUGER
Of Today's Spirit Staff

There was nothing unusual about the play.

In football terminology it's called an option.

The quarterback, in this case Buddy Miley of William Tennent High School, can either flip the ball to a trailing back or he can keep it himself.

Buddy Miley kept it and ran for two yards in Saturday afternoon's Suburban One League game against Plymouth-Whitemarsh at Plymouth Meeting.

It was his final play of the day.

Miley was tackled by several P-W defenders. He did not get up.

Five minutes later Miley was on his way to Sacred Heart Hospital in Norristown.

"HE'S PARALYZED from the chest down," said Tennent coach Bill Juzwiak Sunday night. "He's still got feeling in his arms. The doctors told me he has a compression fracture of a vertebrate on the neck. Right now he's in traction but he's optimistic."

Juzwiak, who formerly coached at Bishop McDevitt of Wyncote and Rensselaer Polytechnic Institute, described the play. "It was just an option. When he got tackled and went down, his head and shoulder hit at the same time. It was a gang tackle and pileup, but it wasn't a dirty play."

Miley was injured at 5:39 of the second period with Tennent trailing

7-6. Tennent eventually lost the game 27-20.

"When I spoke to Buddy at the hospital he apologized for not winning the game," related Juzwiak.

MILEY, WHO IS a 17-year-old senior standing 6-2 and weighing 170, is a transfer from Archbishop Wood. "He

●Please turn to Page 2

Miley's Condition Guarded

Buddy Miley the 6-2, 170 pound quarterback for the William Tennent football team suffered a compression fracture of the cervical vertebrae of his neck in the Plymouth-Whitemarsh game Saturday.

Miley is in guarded condition in the Special Care Unit at the Sacred Heart Hospital in Norristown.

"He was running the option and gained five yards," coach Bill Juzwiak recalled Sunday night, "and when he was hit he fell on his shoulder and head at the same time. Fortunately it was a clean

roughness.

"Buddy was really coming on," Juzwiak continued. "He had sprained his foot earlier in the season, but was over that and was looking sharp in the first series of plays. He was determined to do well this week, and when I visited him in the hospital he said, 'I'm sorry I didn't get a chance to do everything I wanted to.'"

Miley transferred to Tennent from Archbishop Wood where he played on the defensive team and was a top pitcher for the Vikings' base-

Injury To Tennent's Miley Hits Team, Coach Hard

By TERRY BRENNAN
Of Today's Post Staff

Bill Juzwiak stood under a grey sky as Monday afternoon rapidly faced into Monday evening. The grey sky and cold wind reflected Juzwiak's mood.

Everything looked colder, bleaker on the William Tennent campus Monday, two days after Bud Miley was rushed to Sacred Heart Hospital partially paralyzed from his neck down. Juzwiak watched, interested but detached, as the Panther varsity went through a quiet practice session. Their bodies were in Warminster, but their minds were in Norristown.

Miley is in the special care unit at Sacred Heart Hospital, in guarded condition. Monday evening, the Supervisor of Nurses at the hospital listed his condition as "still quite serious."

"HE HAS INJURIES to the cervical vertebrae, and he has no motion at all in his extremities," said the Supervisor.

The Tennent quarterback, injured during Saturday's game against Plymouth-Whitemarsh, had

Miley's spine, small holes were drilled in his skull, and these holes were used to connect the traction.

Assistant principal and athletic director Dave Frye explained that Miley may have shown some unpronounced in the last two days.

"I was just talking to his mother who teaches in the Centennial system, and he told me that Bud had feeling in his stomach and his shoulder," Frye noted.

"BUT HIS CONDITION is still serious. As I understand it, the injury has compressed the fourth and fifth vertebrae in the spinal column, and they are fractured."

Frye had also spoken to Miley's parents since the accident. "Most of their kids are athletically talented, and when you are in this situation, you are geared toward sports.

"They are taking it pretty well," Frye concluded, "but the family, the friends... They know how to take time."

Juzwiak has also been close with the Miley's. "The religious people and Miley's are taking it pretty

also know that it isn't going to be easy," the coach said.

OUTSIDE OF THE family, Juzwiak is probably the most directly involved. He was one of the first to reach Miley as he lay on the Plymouth-Whitemarsh field.

"He wasn't knocked out, he just couldn't move," Juzwiak remembered. "I don't think he was scared, he just kept talking about the game and how he had wanted to do so well.

"Was I scared? Well, it's hard to describe. If I had shown I was scared, then he would have been scared, too. I couldn't let him see

Tennent Students Helping Miley

By DON DAVIS
Intelligencer Sports Editor

William Tennent quarterback Bud Miley, partially paralyzed after suffering an injury in Saturday's football game with Plymouth-Whitemarsh, remains in serious condition at Norristown's Sacred Heart Hospital, special care unit.

"He is still in guarded condition, there has been no change since Monday," said a hospital spokesman this morning.

Miley, a senior at the Warminster school, suffered a compression fracture of the cervical vertebrae of his neck. While running with the ball, Miley landed on his shoulder and head.

The Tennent quarterback does have motion in his shoulders but has been placed in traction to keep his body immobile. It was reported that to relieve the pressure in his spine, small holes were drilled in his skull and the holes were used to connect the traction.

"We're keeping the students apprised of his illness," Assistant principal and athletic director Dave Frye said this morning. "The kids are beginning to raise money and try to help anyway they can.

"The kids are signing a big autographed card to send to him.

"The latest we had heard was that there was increased feeling in his chest, stomach and back. Things are progressing."

A dedicated football player, Miley was still concerned about the team immediately following his injury. "I'm sorry I didn't get a chance to do everything I wanted to," he told his

coach, Bill Juzwiak, in the hospital on Sunday.

Now the team and the school are taking time to care about him.

WE'RE THINKIN' OF YA BUDDY—William Tennent students (from left) Jeanette Oldroyd, Carolyn Craig and Beverly Reiss take time to sign a gigantic card for Buddy Miley, injured quarterback. The card, with over 500 signatures, was taken to the athlete Tuesday night along with a tape from the football team. Miley is still in a "guarded condition."

Card Tells Him 'Get Up'

Miley Improves Little By Little

By DON DAVIS
Intelligencer Sports Editor

Buddy Miley waves good-bye to his football coach Sunday night.

It may not sound like much, but for a young man in a hospital bed, partially paralyzed, it is a treat for everyone.

"He's in real good spirits," said William Tennent coach Bill Juzwiak following his son to Sacred Heart Hospital Tuesday evening.

Miley, a senior at the Warminster school, was injured on Saturday in a foot-

ball game. Following a tackle, the player was left paralyzed. Day by day, however, he has continued to make slight improvements though the hospital continues to list him in "guarded condition."

'More Movement'

"He has a little more movement in his arms," said Juzwiak. "He waved good-bye through a wire hoop for the game. This time they (play hospital) moved his head while he was a head for us."

Juzwiak says his hospital room is in "constant pain," but he expects to come out of

terback a speedy recovery. Before 50 students signed the card.

"He needs people to help him to get up," said Juzwiak. "The tape told him to get up, the card said to get up. The tape really did a lot of good. He has on a lot of occasions, encouraged them. This time they (play hospital people) moved his head while he was a head for us."

Juzwiak says his hospital is in "constant pain," but

Juzwiak says that he was told that it will be his pride that pulls him through. "He just said 'get up' when he had to have to go

Game Ball

At practice on the William Tennent field, Juzwiak says that "there's a lot of emotion. They all want to win this one," he said. "They want to give him the game ball."

Everything's optimistic and Juzwiak, "I know he's going to get well."

Perhaps the coach knew when he saw his star wave goodbye...

INJURED — William Tennent quarterback Bud Miley gets set to pass in game early this season.

Newspaper clippings.

SEVEN

Am I Paralyzed?

Jimmy led Donnie Schultz down the steep stairwell, ignoring the chin-up bar over the bottom step that the boys always used to swing from. Weak light seeped through the basement windows onto odds and ends of drab furniture. With Bob off on his own and Buddy upstairs, Jimmy had the space to himself now and enjoyed the privacy, even if a hard rain would leave the floor ankle deep in water. But on this day there was only the usual clutter underfoot: uncollected laundry, baseball gloves, and toys from the previous Christmas. As Donnie looked over his shoulder, Jimmy set up the Bell & Howell projector on a table and attached a movie reel to the spindle. When he switched it on, a square of light appeared on the wall. Into it steps Buddy, his lean body crouched over center as the Plymouth Whitemarsh defense settles into position.

The ball is snapped.

Buddy drops back, pivots, and turns up field.

A hole opens up in the line.

Buddy slips through it but is upended after a short gain and disappears beneath a swarm of converging tacklers.

Jimmy switched the projector off.

The two boys just sat there until Donnie said, "So that was it? That was how he did it?"

Jimmy shrugged and replied, "Well, yeah . . ."

Jimmy backed up the film that the school had given the Mileys and played it again. "Look. See how Buddy dips his head? See how the other guys come in? And the way Buddy lands?"

Donnie could not think of what else to say, so he only said, "Wow."

Whatever else Jimmy would remember, it would be this: Something very wrong had been in the air that day. Given that he was only eleven, he could not fully grasp what had happened, only that "all hell seemed to break loose" and the adults that surrounded him were consumed with panic. Bert had called from Sacred Heart Hospital, but had been too overcome to speak, breaking down as he uttered the words, "Buddy is . . ." But Bob took the receiver from him and told Rosemarie, "Buddy is in the hospital. It's pretty bad." When her sister-in-law Eileen Miley heard what happened—that Buddy had a possible broken neck—she immediately called her two sisters, who were nuns in Ocean City, New Jersey. Eileen asked them to pray for her nephew that evening at mass. At the Miley house, Eileen hugged Rosemarie and gathered the youngest of the children, Patti, Linda, and Jimmy.

"Get down on your knees," she told them.

They did.

And she began a rosary.

"The First Sorrowful Mystery, the Agony of Jesus in the Garden . . ."

The children bowed their heads as their aunt began with the Apostles' Creed, the beads entwined in her fingers as she held the crucifix in her hands. "I believe in God, the Father almighty, creator of heaven and earth. I believe in Jesus Christ, His only Son, our Lord. He was conceived by the power of the Holy Spirit and born of the Virgin Mary. He suffered under Pontius Pilate, was crucified, died, and was buried. He descended to the dead. On the third day He rose again. He ascended into heaven and is seated at the right hand of the Father. He will come again to judge the living and the dead. I believe in the Holy Spirit, the holy Catholic Church, the communion of saints, the forgiveness of sins, the resurrection of the body, and life everlasting. Amen."

Somewhere beyond his line of vision in the emergency room at Sacred Heart Hospital, Buddy overheard someone say in a low voice, "We'll just have to see. There's a chance he won't live through the night." So . . . that explained why no one had looked in on him for what seemed to be hours: *They're waiting for me to die.* He had the overwhelming sense that he was encased from the neck down in hard cement, unable to move any of his appendages upon command. Yet he still had some feeling, even if it reminded him of being pricked by "a thousand needles." Searching the room with his eyes, he looked over at his brother Bob and told him he was thirsty. Bob found a cup of water and held it to his lips. Buddy jutted his chin forward, sipped from it, and asked, "Am I paralyzed? Bob? Am I paralyzed?" Bob did not know what to say, but remembers that he was consumed by dread, the escalating sense that none of their lives would ever again be the same. Bert remembers even less, just that he pounded his head against the wall in the adjoining room as a priest stood by his side. Someone later had asked him to sign a form, but he was shaking so hard that he could not hold a pen in his hand. Bert says, "It was a dark day."

Whatever could go wrong did go wrong for Buddy in the hours that followed the injury. Given the extreme distress he had exhibited on the field, he should have been triaged by the EMT and paramedic, immobilized, and sent to a regional trauma center. But that did not happen. According to players who were there, well-intentioned hands rolled Buddy over on his back, removed his helmet, and hoisted him up onto a stretcher. None of the protocols that were in place for dealing with a spinal-cord injury were followed, including something as simple as the immediate application of ice to control swelling. Exactly why it was presumed that Buddy had a broken leg will never be known—the EMT "run report" and the hospital records have long been discarded. But as Tim Erlacher, the injured P-W player, and Bert both say, that is precisely what the EMT alerted Sacred Heart Hospital, then a small hospital that was not staffed to handle a spinal-cord problem with the same efficiency as a trauma center. Consequently, an emergency-room aide stripped Buddy out of his uniform jersey by removing it over his head instead of cutting it off. Rosemarie shakes her head and sighs, "What can I say?

Contrary to what had been suspected, Buddy had sustained a grave injury to his spinal column, an intricate system of thirty-three vertebrae designed to surround and protect a cord of supple tissue the diameter of an index finger that extends from the base of the skull to the lower back. At the very top of the spinal column are seven cervical vertebrae, followed by twelve thoracic, five lumbar, five sacral, and four coccyx. In between each vertebra are peripheral nerves that branch out into the body and carry commands from the brain to the limbs—*Pick up that cup!*—or respond to outward stimuli that trigger nerve impulses back through the spinal cord to the brain—*Ouch! That stung!* In the event that the spinal cord is damaged, the signals to the brain are interrupted, with a loss of function below the point of impairment, which is why the higher up the spinal column an injury occurs, the more catastrophic the outcome can be. An injury at C3 is commonly fatal in that it impacts breathing.

While Buddy would have some issues that indicated damage at C3, including a weakened diaphragm that would cause him to run out of air before he completed sentences and a predisposition to pneumonia because of his inability to cough effectively, X-rays revealed he suffered severe damage at C4 and C5, which control the arms and legs. Imagine an automobile that had an engine but no axles.

"Hold his head! Hold his head!" commanded the neurosurgeon that had been called in. The big concern now was the degree of swelling within the spinal cord, by then lodged between the jagged edges of the vertebrae. Given that Carmen Frangiosa had observed Buddy move his upper body on the field, it is conceivable that had he received cautious handling on the field, he could have later recovered some level of function over an extended rehabilitation. But no one would ever be able to say with any certainty when the possibility of a positive outcome was extinguished, if Buddy had been doomed at the point of impact, or if additional damage had occurred in the immediate aftermath. Given corticosteroids at the hospital to curtail swelling, he was placed in traction, with ten-pound weights attached to two bolts drilled in the back of his skull, and strapped into a Stryker frame, which enabled him to be turned front and back and side to side to prevent bedsores. Tears slid down his cheeks as Rosemarie walked into the ICU.

"Mom," he said, "I'm paralyzed."

Rosemarie placed her hand on his and replied in a composed voice, "Bud, it'll be fine."

Getting to the hospital had been a challenge for Rosemarie, who was driven by Eileen and accompanied by a friend, Flos Lutz. Uncertain of how to get to Sacred Heart Hospital, Eileen spotted Mercy Suburban Hospital and stopped there for directions. The women were wild with anxiety, the three of them searching for street signs as they speculated on what would happen to Buddy. When they finally got to Sacred Heart Hospital, Rosemarie saw how pale Bert looked and remembers hearing him explain, "It was a clean hit." But Rosemarie was not prepared for the surge of emotion that welled up in her when she looked down at Buddy in that Stryker frame, rivulets of blood flowing from the site of where the two holes had been drilled into his skull. She told herself, *I cannot let him see me cry.* None of her children ever had, with the exception of that day in November 1963, when she'd stood over her ironing board as Walter Cronkite removed his glasses and said, "From Dallas, Texas, the flash apparently official. President Kennedy died at one central standard time . . . two eastern standard time . . . some thirty-eight minutes ago." Bob had come home from school that day and had seen her standing there weeping for the fallen JFK, the first Irish Catholic ever to ascend to the presidency. But while Rosemarie did not let Buddy see her cry that day at Sacred Heart Hospital, tears welled in her eyes as she sat in a rear pew at the small chapel there and prayed.

Hail Mary, full of grace.
Our Lord is with thee.
Blessed art thou among women,
And blessed is the fruit of thy womb,
Jesus.
Holy Mary, Mother of God,
Pray for us sinners,
Now and at the hour of our death.
Amen.
And then: *Please, Lord. Let him walk.*

Sitting along the walls of the hospital corridors were scattered groups of somber Tennent players. Coach Juzwiak stood in the waiting room with the Mileys, their faces etched in worry. Frangiosa even stopped by, but to see his teammate Erlacher, not Buddy. Erlacher had sat in the emergency room for what seemed forever as doctors occasionally stopped by and assured him, "Hang in there. We'll get to you." Not until his father dropped by later was the delay explained. "Just relax," the elder Erlacher said. "The kid they brought in with you has a busted neck." But Frangiosa was unaware of any of that as he looked in on Erlacher and asked him if he was okay.

Erlacher told him, "Yeah," but nodded to where the doctors were working with Buddy. "But this is bad over there."

"I know," Frangiosa said. "He has a broken arm or something."

"Noooooo."

"What happened?"

Erlacher shook his head. "It's not good."

Frangiosa walked into the waiting room and found Bob Miley, who looked at him mournfully and said, "Carmen, Buddy is paralyzed." The force of those words slammed into the young player "like a punch in the jaw." Quickly, he did an inventory of the events of the day: *It had been a hard hit, but no harder than any other. It had been bad, you could see that. But paralyzed? My God!* Told by his coach that Buddy had a broken arm, Frangiosa had allowed himself to slide back into the rhythm of the game, which Plymouth Whitemarsh would end up winning, 27–20. He even looked across the line at the new Tennent quarterback, Pace Gonnam, and said, "I'm tracking you down next, pal!" Frangiosa remembers the young sophomore was "scared shitless." But in the weeks that followed, it was Frangiosa who would feel tracked, and who would wonder why it had been Buddy and not him who had been injured on the play.

How could this have happened?

He turned to his father. "Dad, I don't know. I'm not dealing with this thing."

The World War II veteran looked at him, worried by the deep

turmoil that his son was in. "What are you talking about? When you walk out on the battlefield, you never know who is going to get hurt. Or killed. Sometimes it just happens, just like this just happened. Did you plan it? No."

Word of what had happened spread through the two schools on Monday. A headline that day in the sports section of the local paper announced, "QB Is Paralyzed in Tennent Game." Juzwiak fielded interviews with reporters but remembers thinking then, *What do I do now? Quit?* But he continued coaching and his players continued playing, swept up in the schoolwide campaign to lend Buddy support and encouragement. At P-W, some players did drop off the team because of what happened, either told to do so by their parents or just suddenly concerned for their own safety. Sensing the uneasy mood that had settled over his team, Coach Charters called his players in a circle and told them Buddy could just as easily have injured himself by falling off his bicycle or from being hit the wrong way by a wave at the shore. Charters arranged for his players to bus over to the hospital, but Grant Hudson could not bring himself to go, an omission that for years would leave him thinking he had behaved as "kind of a coward."

Outwardly, Buddy impressed the P-W players as being in surprisingly high spirits. As they shuffled into his room in small groups, their eyes cast downward or on the profusion of tubes and wires attached to his still body, he greeted them with a wide grin, as if any second he would get up out of the bed, eye a ball that his teammates had given him, and say, "Toss that over here." But that would always be an ability Buddy had, the way he had of putting people at ease. Mike Dippolito found this to be the case when he came into the room and Buddy asked, "Who is number forty-two?" Immediately, Dippolito began to redden, unsure why he had been asked to identify himself. He had played with Buddy on the Little Quakers.

Dippolito told him he was No. 42. "Remember me, Bud?" From the Little Quakers? Mike?"

"Oh, yeah." Buddy smiled at Dippolito and reminded him how he had batted down what had been Buddy's final touchdown pass.

Dippolito relaxed.

"Good play," Buddy told him. "Grab my hand, pick it up, and shake it."

Whenever visitors dropped by the hospital—and they did so frequently in those early days—Buddy told them that his injury was a temporary setback, that he would be healed by spring and back on the field. He would play his senior year and go on to college, just as he had always planned. Of course, that would not be possible, not by that spring or any spring. While his neurosurgeon had explained that it would be a year before they would know what functions Buddy would regain, if any, he told Bert and Rosemarie that the odds of that happening were less than favorable. Their son would be a quadriplegic. Someone would have to care for him. But there was never any question where he would go or who would take care of him. Whatever happened in the years ahead, Rosemarie would see to it that Buddy would get the around-the-clock attention that only someone who loved him so dearly could provide. She knew it would be hard on Bert and her other children, especially the youngest of them, Jimmy, who would slip even deeper into the background.

Those early days would remain a blur to Jimmy. Joanne, his oldest sister, had been house-sitting somewhere, and Jimmy and Linda stayed with her that initial evening. Confused, the two asked Joanne, "What is a broken neck? Is Buddy going to be okay?" Jimmy did not see Buddy for a few days, and he stood in the back when he finally did, behind his parents, Bob, and his sisters. Seeing Buddy again and hearing him talk was a relief, even if it was startling to his young eyes the way they had him hooked up in that Stryker frame. While

Buddy stopped eating and spiraled into a depression in the hospital, Jimmy found him upbeat whenever he would go see him, so Jimmy would be upbeat, too, thinking, *It's a just break. Players get 'em all the time. It'll heal.* Not until later did he begin to understand the implications of the word *paralyzed,* when a friend stopped by the room to see Buddy and picked up a football that was lying on a chair. With Buddy facedown in the Stryker frame, the friend touched the back of his leg with the ball.

"Do you feel that?" the friend said.

"No," Buddy said.

The friend lifted the ball. "Do you feel that?"

"Yes," Buddy said.

Jimmy looked over at Buddy and under his breath said, "Oh, shit."

. . . . .

Buddy and Karen on graduation day, 1974.

CREDIT: *1974 PER ANNOS*, WILLIAM TENNENT SENIOR HIGH SCHOOL

. . . . .

EIGHT

Butterfly Kisses

She would ask him, "Where would you like to go, Buddy?"

And he would say, "Somewhere warm. The beach."

And he would close his eyes and she would take him there, the two of them together strolling along the edge of the surf. The day would always be perfect, hot but not too hot, and a sea breeze would bring with it the scent of saltwater, which blended with the aroma of the coconut oil he had rubbed on her back. Squawking gulls would arc overhead in lazy patterns as the couple walked, hand in hand, the waves spilling at their feet. To cool off, they would run into the water, splashing this way and that, and dive over a collapsing breaker. Then they would dry themselves, sit down in the warm sand, and huddle beneath a large towel until the sun began to dip over the horizon. She would lean her head on his shoulder.

He would open his eyes again and she would be there, looking up at him from the floor of his hospital room. Strapped upside down in the Stryker frame, an awkward position that would always leave him with the sensation that he was falling, he would gaze at her and be carried away, if not to the beach then to someplace else where he could lay down his pain. But it was not just what she said that so enchanted him. It was her voice—its hypnotic quality soothed him in ways no therapy or pharmaceutical ever could. On her part, he always evinced a keen interest in whatever she had to say and would leave her feeling seen—and safe. Spending those weeks at the Philadelphia Naval Hospital had equipped her with an ability to look beyond the injury and see only the man. And that is who Karen Shields saw: Buddy.

But they were so young then, so inexperienced in the inexplicable ways of the heart. Karen remembers that while she had been disappointed he had not called her that Saturday evening, a part of her also looked upon it with relief. Were they to begin seeing each other outside of school, it concerned her that they would have nothing in common. Sports held no interest for her, and she wondered if he had ever opened a book. Plus, she was not so sure she wanted a boyfriend, which she suspected had the potential to be smothering. But she clearly felt an attraction between them, a pull that was gravitational, and the feelings it stirred in her were hard to deny. So as she turned off the light by her bed, she told herself that she would look up Buddy at school on Monday.

Amid the panic and rumors that circulated through the halls at Tennent—that Buddy was paralyzed and perhaps even near death—Karen tried to piece together what had happened from the conversations she overheard. She looked for Bob Miley but did not see him that day, so she just assumed that the injury had indeed been serious. When Bob did return to his classes later in the week, she found herself standing with him one day outside his room and asked how Buddy was doing. She gave Bob her name and said, "Tell him I am thinking of him." A week or so later, Bob found her and said that Buddy had asked her to drop by the hospital. So one day she got into her lime-green Ford Pinto and did just that. She wore a blue dress with red flowers and her favorite red platform heels. At the hospital, Buddy introduced her to his mother and some other family members, who left them for what they would call "our first date." Immediately, they slipped into easy conversation and laughter, as if they were old friends who had found each other again. Whatever apprehensions she had vanished. When a nurse came in to "flip" him two hours later, Buddy asked Karen, "Can you stay?"

She began going up to the Sacred Heart Hospital daily. Given free rein by her parents that senior year, she would get off school around noon, work for a few hours with a wedding photographer in a job that the school had lined up for her, and go to the hospital, seldom eating dinner at home. By arrangement with the hospital staff, she would be there for two "facedown rotations," which is to say she would spend two hours on her back, another two on her feet, and a final two on her back. With her head propped up on a pillow, she would lie on the floor and look up at him and they would go off on "vacation," as they used to refer to it, far from the pain that would leave him shuddering with spasms. That pain—those needles—would come upon him in waves and leave him weeping. And yet . . . perhaps it was an encouraging sign. He told himself—and told Karen—that he would eventually get even more feeling back, that he would not just become ambulatory again but well enough to play ball and go to college. But whatever plans he once had now included Karen, even if— and he always said this with a preening chuckle—he would inevitably be surrounded on campus by hot-looking girls. She laughed along with him whenever he said this, unaware he would never walk again. At seventeen, there are no absolutes, only infinite possibilities.

"Boy, you look like you are in another world," she said as she came to see him one day. "What's going on in that head of yours? What happened here today?"

"Is it cold outside? I've been cold all day. I had them bring me extra blankets. I can't seem to get warm."

"Yeah. There is a chill in the air today. It's probably the first time I actually needed my jacket. Are you still cold?"

Grimly, Buddy nodded. "Yeah. Are the blankets covering my feet? My legs are cold."

Karen checked the thermostat in the room—seventy-eight. Keeping warm would always be a problem for Buddy, whose paralysis obstructed his ability to produce adequate body heat. Gray winter days were especially hard on him, which is why he always pictured himself at the beach, the sun beating down on his bare shoulders. Karen set the thermostat at eighty and began rearranging his blankets, tucking them underneath his legs and shoulders in an effort to seal in whatever heat he generated. Some color began to return to his pale face. But she could sense something else was at work on him today, that not just the cold accounted for his mood. She placed a hand on his cheek and asked again, "Now tell me, what's been going on here today?"

"It's just so good to see you, Karen. I missed you today. I was getting worried that you weren't going to come by. It's just been a rough one. Seems like I've been waiting for you all day. They're trying to get me to sit up, so they just came in and cranked up my head until I got dizzy and passed out. Pissed me off." He paused. "Will you get my glasses? They forgot to put them back on."

"Do you want me to exercise your legs?" She adjusted his glasses on the bridge of his nose. "Maybe it'll warm you up."

Buddy grinned. "Yeah. Would you?"

Weeks had passed by then. With an open book propped up on her knee, Karen would sit outside the room until any other visitors had left. Eileen would remember wondering early on who "the very, very pretty blond girl" was, and how she sat vigil at the hospital "almost as long as we did." From 10:00 A.M. until 3:00 P.M., Rose-marie would be there each day, usually by herself. Years later, she explains, "Everyone had to get back to their lives." The older siblings were also always there—Bob, Rosemarie, and Joanne—and even the younger ones came by, Patti, Linda, and Jimmy. Friends also stopped by to fill him in on what was happening at school. Whenever Karen was there, they would glance at her and then at Buddy, who would introduce her not as his girlfriend but as "Karen, a friend from school." When it came to his affections for her, Buddy kept her in a private place, if only to stave off what he would call "the bullshit" he suspected he would get from other people: *Bud, get serious. You know she'll end up leaving. What then?* But whenever he and Karen were alone, a far more open and tender side would emerge, the part that would ask a nurse to bring Karen a yellow rose because she had once told him she liked them.

One of the friends who dropped by was Pat Delaney, who had been a teammate with Buddy on the Little Quakers—the one who had wanted to "crack" him for cutting his shoelaces. Squat in build with a hard-nosed, working-class bearing, Delaney had gone on to play at P-W, only to be tossed off the team the week before the Ten-nent game when he got into a scuffle with Charters. The two were always at odds. The friction came to a head when Delaney asked to "challenge" for the starting job and was denied, which led to heated words and some shoving. Consequently, Delaney spent that Satur-day at a golf course and did not become aware of what had hap-pened to Buddy until he saw Dippolito in homeroom. "Dippy" had told him, "Your buddy got taken out on a stretcher. It didn't look good." Delaney began stopping by Sacred Heart Hospital to watch *Monday Night Football,* bringing a six-pack of beer. When visiting hours were over, he would climb under a table and hide. With Buddy up-side down in the Stryker frame, Delaney would crack open a beer and describe the action in the game as Howard Cosell sparred with Frank Gifford and Don Meredith.

"Give me a beer," Buddy said.

Delaney replied, "Buddy, I can't. Jesus Christ, you'll get me in trouble. I shouldn't even be in here now."

But not everyone who dropped by was so at ease. Girls from school would stop in for a visit, giddy with excitement, only to stand there in stunned silence when they saw him, now gaunt with an unhealthy pallor. Some never came back. Tennent teammate Bob McCarney remembered that even as Buddy would try to lighten the atmosphere with humor, he would also slip into a dejected state, his voice becoming halting and his eyes welling with tears as he described his inability to brush his teeth. Seeing him was a dose of reality that none of his peers were prepared for, especially his old friend Guy Driesbach. At Staunton Military Academy in Virginia that fall, Driesbach had received newspaper clippings from home chronicling what had happened to Buddy, who just a few years ago had been running with him with wild abandon through that cornfield. But not until he came home for the Christmas break and saw Buddy did "it hit home," as he remembered. He went into the bathroom and threw up.

Unsteadily, he came out of the bathroom and lowered his eyes. *Good God,* he wondered, *how could this have happened?*

Buddy looked at him and asked, "Are you okay?"

However compromised he had become physically, Buddy developed acute powers of observation. Footsteps echoed in the corridor outside his room all day every day, but he knew which ones belonged to Karen by the way that her shoes clicked along the linoleum floor. Whenever he had other visitors and she would sit in the corner with a book, he would know exactly what page she was on when they were alone again. Amazed, she once asked, "How in the world did you know that?" He told her, "I counted each page you turned." She would curl up with him in his bed and place a leg over his, the weight of which helped quell the spasms that would overtake him. When she departed at the end of the evening, she would leave behind traces of mascara on his pillowcase—or, as he would call them, "butterfly kisses." As a security guard walked Karen to her car, Buddy would try to sleep, his eyes fixed on the pattern of small holes that had been drilled into the tile ceiling above his head. He would count them: *One . . . two . . . three . . . four . . . five . . . six.* There were four hundred twenty-six of them.

The attachment between Buddy and her daughter concerned Janet Shields, who says, "She did not have me in her corner on this. I understood she was trying to help someone, but it seemed extreme for such a young girl to be so involved with taking care of a person she did not know that well." Bob Shields had the same concerns and remembers that he wondered, *What is it with this?* But both prided themselves on giving their children space, and they did that with Karen, who planned to attend college when she graduated from Tennent in the spring. Ultimately—or so her parents believed—Buddy and Karen would go their separate ways, if only because Bob was planning to leave the navy and take a private-sector job. Though an opportunity had presented itself in Pennsylvania, it seemed likely they would be off to either Florida or New Mexico, which would provide them with an excuse to move Karen away from Warminster—and Buddy. Karen held out hope that they would remain in the Philadelphia area and told Buddy so. But Buddy seemed fine with it and said that their plans would remain the same: She would go to college and he would undergo rehab.

But reality began settling in before a decision on the future ever came to pass. Greeted by the clang of Sue Schultz banging on a pot a few doors away, Buddy was dropped off back home by ambulance on Christmas Eve, only to be returned the following day for a few more weeks at Sacred Heart Hospital. By his eighteenth birthday in January he was home for good, at which point Bert and Rosemarie moved to the sofa. With Buddy in a hospital bed in their bedroom, the small house became even smaller, the narrow hall always crowded with visitors. Karen still came over, but now not without calling ahead. Gone were the long conversations they once had, the sweet intimacies. She would stay for less than a half hour, during which their expressions of affection became whispered. To help pitch in during that spring of 1974, Karen would take Jimmy to his baseball games and sit in the bleachers. She was unaware just how imperiled her own health would soon become.

Unexplained symptoms from her childhood had come back the spring of her senior year. While she did not have a fever, she began experiencing sharp pains in her lower abdomen and such fatigue that she fell asleep in class. Her mother remembers that Karen used to wake up screaming. Initially, the diagnosis was "a female issue" connected to her period. But a doctor at the Philadelphia Naval Hospital discovered that she had a duplicate kidney system, which caused urine to flow from her bladder back into her kidney and produced a buildup in toxins that led to inflammation and swelling. Surgery was immediately scheduled. The operation took six hours, during which she was given four units of blood. Sedated that initial week due to extensive internal bleeding, she remembers that when she woke up, she asked her parents, "Did Buddy call?" and then drifted off again. But three weeks passed and no one from the Miley house had called, even just to check in with her parents to see how she had come through surgery. She wondered to herself, *What happened?*

She did not betray how wounded she was when she saw Buddy again, nor did she even bring the subject up. But something had changed. Buddy was standoffish when she came to see him, even offended in an odd way that she had not been in contact with him. It occurred to her later that he had used her hospital stay to disconnect from her, that perhaps he "had seen the handwriting on the wall" that he would not recover and employed this hiatus as an opportunity to let her go. But when she came to see him again and inform him that her parents would be moving to Florida, he looked at her from his bed, became choked up, and said, "I knew that was going to happen." Tears flowed from his eyes—and hers. It seemed as if they sat there for hours, not knowing what to do or say, until Buddy gathered himself and drew up what Karen remembers as "a very practical plan." Suddenly, it was if he were the quarterback again, kneeling down in the huddle.

One day he would come for her. Wherever she was, he would sweep her up into his arms and take her away.

But he would not come for her until he could walk again and be a man in full. It would happen. But it would take time, perhaps even years. And it would be unfair of him to ask her not to see anyone else.

So . . . they were not breaking up. But she should not contact him. That would be too hard.

She told him she would be there when he came.

Graduation Day at William Tennent High School, class of 1974, was held on a scorching June day. On one side of the stage, Karen sat in a wheelchair, a precaution due to the heat. In his wheelchair on the other side of the stage sat Buddy, who had been tutored during the spring and received his diploma. When Buddy had told her in their parting conversation not good-bye but "See ya later," there had seemed to be in his eyes an appeal to her to stay. But on Graduation Day, he glanced the other way when she waved at him and, at the end of the ceremony, was encircled by a wall of friends. Karen stood up from her wheelchair and walked to the car with her parents. In the backseat, her eyes shimmered with tears as she wondered what would become of him, and if she would ever again feel so loved by a simple look.

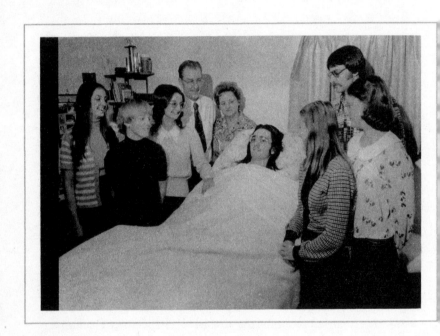

Home again.

NINE

· · · · ·

Orange

Early on a June morning, the front gate at the Johnsville Naval Air Station swung open, and the backhoe that Dave Heilbrun had asked for loomed before his eyes, the engine coughing and wheezing as it chugged out onto Street Road. Lining up a backhoe had not been easy—no one seemed to have one—but somehow Heilbrun discovered that an old clunker was out at the base. When he looked into it, the by-the-book commander told him no, only to be circumvented by a subordinate who later contacted Heilbrun and told him, "Okay, you can have it, just come by Saturday at five A.M. with somebody who knows how to drive it." So Heilbrun found "a kid from South Philly" to sit behind the wheel, showed up at the appointed hour, and began the trip to the Miley house, where they drove up on the lawn and began digging the foundation of what would become "Buddy's room." Hours passed and they were still digging when suddenly the South Philly kid passed out from the fumes that belched from the exhaust pipe. They revived him, but when he gathered himself, he discovered that he had lost his wallet. They looked and looked but never found it.

The thirty-three-year-old Heilbrun became acquainted with the Mileys through a friend who had told him of their predicament. Cut loose from his job as a pilot at United Airlines during the 1973 recession, he had been piecing together a living doing design work, the rudiments of which he had learned from some architectural classes he had taken as an undergraduate at Penn State. The Mileys had hoped to build an addition for Buddy, so Heilbrun produced a set of drawings for it. But it soon became clear that the Mileys could not afford what appeared certain to be a $20,000 job. Bert said sadly, "Honestly, I'm in just no position to swing it." But Heilbrun remembers that he had come to like the Mileys—Buddy in particular. While he had only had some brief conversations with him, Buddy had tapped a place inside Heilbrun, perhaps the same wellspring of compassion that once compelled his grandfather to aspire to missionary work before he was waylaid by tuberculosis. Heilbrun told Bert he would get back to them. He reworked his drawings and began calling around.

Heilbrun would discover just how giving his fellow man can be in the face of tragedy. With the blueprints that he had labored on during the Memorial Day weekend in hand—somewhat scaled down from the original versions he showed Bert—he contacted his acquaintances in the construction field and explained what he needed, and why. "What would it cost to have carpenters frame this out?" he asked contractor Bob Held. Surprisingly, Held got back to him and said the carpenters would do it for free, just as the masons and plumbers and electricians would. No one asked Heilbrun for a dime for supplies or labor. Workmen swarmed the house, pouring concrete, hammering nails, and installing unique features, such as a five-hundred-pound ceiling track so Buddy could be ferried from his bed to a chair or the bathroom. New volunteers showed up every Saturday to lend a hand. By August, the room was finished and Heilbrun began looking for furnishings. At a nearby outlet, he spotted a cabinet he liked and explained the situation to the manager.

"Can you donate it?" Heilbrun asked.

"Well . . . ," the manager said with some hesitancy. "We really don't do that."

The manager paused and asked him to follow him to the storeroom. There, he told Heilbrun that he could only let him have "a damaged piece," whereupon he picked up a hammer and tapped the back of the model Heilbrun had been eyeing.

"There!" the manager said. "It's damaged. Get it out of here."

Equipped with a telephone conferencing system, whirlpool, and central air and heating that Buddy could adjust to swings in his body temperature, the new room was not exactly the "bachelor's pad" that Rosemarie told people. But it did give Buddy something he had not had in the back bedroom—a window and two doors. The window would provide him a landscape to look out on: big trees that would change color with the seasons; school buses that would pick up children at the beginning of the day and drop them off at the end of it; and cars that would drive by and acknowledge him with a beep of the horn or a casual wave. But the two doors would prove to be even more of a blessing, enabling him to regain some small piece of privacy. One led to the outside, which allowed visitors to drop by without drawing the attention of his parents and siblings. The other opened onto the living room, and Rosemarie slid it closed whenever Buddy wanted to have a private chat. When Bert passed by and slid it back open, Buddy would shout, "Close that door!"

But his father would just walk away.

And Buddy would seethe: *There he goes, eavesdropping again.* Friends would remember how they would be in there with Buddy, and Bert would be in the living room with the TV on. He would stand up, stride across to the set, and lower the sound just enough so he could overhear the conversation that was taking place. Buddy would yell, "Stop listening!"

In a certain way, it was as if the Mileys were soldiers huddled together in a foxhole: united by duty—and love—but worn down by unremitting stress. In the case of Bert, the strained relationship he had with Buddy before the injury only worsened as the years passed. They seldom spoke, yet were forever pissed off at each other: Bert, say, at how long Buddy always wore his hair, or some other act of rebellion that undermined his authority; Buddy at the way Bert lived at the top of his lungs, barking at whoever disagreed with him or had an idea of his own. God, it killed Buddy—just killed him—when his father snapped at Rosemarie. Had he been able to get up out of that bed, Buddy would surely have taken a swing at him. But Bert would calm down, sit on the sofa, and brood, or go to work or head up to the field, the very picture of the American patriarch thwarted, in the grasp of unspoken heartache and unable to repair what he would years later refer to as "the big problem we had in the other room." But there would be no fixing Buddy and he knew that, even if he would always be upbeat whenever someone asked him if there had been any progress. Inside, he had curled up in a ball.

It was not that Rosemarie did not absorb the crushing weight of these same tensions, but she was better at hiding it, just as she was better at hiding her tears. Rarely did she lose her cool, grab her keys, and announce that she had had enough. On one such occasion—and she is not sure exactly what set her off—she slammed the door behind her and got in her car, only to discover it was out of gas. So she just sat there, her head propped against the steering wheel, and remembered that day years before when, as a young woman, she packed up Bob in the stroller and walked back to her childhood home, away from whatever her husband had done that day—or had not done. Rose Quinn, her mother—or Nana as the children would call her—had given her lunch that day, told her to go home, and shooed her back to the world she now occupied, no longer accented by beaming servicemen and lovely gowns. In the years of struggle that would ensue, Rosemarie would draw inspiration from Nana, who had stood up under the pressure of taking care of poor Frankie, the angelic Down syndrome boy who was handed to her at the hospital as if he were unworthy of breath.

But Nana would not hear of it, just as Rosemarie would not hear of leaving Buddy to be cared for by someone else for any extended period. "Women are just stronger than men," Rosemarie says, her admiration for Nana stirring in her voice. She remembers how Nana had set up an "office" in her basement for Frankie, equipped with a desk, typewriter, pencils, and crayons. Through his twenties and thirties, he played there with the Miley children. The kids loved him, and he loved them. Whenever any of them incited the ire of an adult, Frankie stepped forward and shouldered the blame. Whenever they squabbled, he would get between them and plead, "No! No! No!" Any exhibition of discord scared him. Nana was strict with him when she had to be, but always loving, careful to keep him close at her side and out from underfoot of strangers. Ultimately, Rosemarie would come to look upon Buddy with the same surpassing fidelity. When years later she would overhear Bert use the word *problem* in association with Buddy, she lowered her voice and said simply, "He was my boy."

Given the unstinting, year in and year out care that Rosemarie provided him, Buddy would elevate her to the station of a deity—"Saint Rosemarie," he would always cheerfully call her. The days had an engulfing sameness to them, beginning at 7:30 A.M. and not ending until 11:00 P.M. Because Buddy could not feed himself, Rosemarie did it for him—cereal or an egg for breakfast, a soup or sandwich for lunch, and whatever she happened to be cooking for dinner. She bathed him. She brushed his teeth. And she dressed him. To stave off bedsores, she turned him on his side in bed at two-hour intervals. When the weather was agreeable, she would help him into his wheelchair and sit him outside in the sun. When it was not, she would sit him in a chair by the window. He could not dial the telephone, so she did it for him, just as she turned the pages of the occasional book he would read or changed the channel on the TV set. One of his favorite shows became *General Hospital,* which in the 1970s had America transfixed by the torrid love affair between Luke and Laura. Whenever he had the show on, Rosemarie would tease him. The light byplay between the two would allay the boredom that settled over the house. Occasionally, someone would be dancing on television, and Rosemarie would whirl across the room, the spring back in her step. "This is how we did it back in the old days!" she would say. And Buddy would say, "Okay, Mom," and grin, just as he did whenever she reminded him of the handsome young men who used to squire her onto the ballroom floor.

Oh . . . and one of them even wrote her a poem—a sweet boy . . . became a writer.

She found it one day when she was cleaning out a drawer and read it aloud.

"Oh, Mom," Buddy said with a chuckle. "He was feeding you a line and you fell for it!"

"No," Rosemarie said. "The boys loved me. I was cute!"

However exhausting the days where, her other children always pitched in one way or another. Patti, the hairdresser, showed up at the house every day, either to assist Rosemarie with some of the chores she had with Buddy or see to it that his hair was trimmed and in place. And his contact lenses—she helped him with those. Whatever else he had been deprived of, he could not let go of his vanity, and he had a dogged desire to always look . . . perfect. "That was his thing," Patti says. On days when the pain was bothering him, he could become irritable and snarl at Patti as she stood over him with her clippers, "Come on, do it the right way!" And Patti would reply, not giving an inch, "Okay then, you do it!" But that was just the way she was, loving yet forceful when it came to working with Buddy. Whenever she had to get him in the shower, she would wrap him in a towel and say, "Okay, get in the shower. Hurry up. Get in and get out." Patti remembers, "I just had a personality where I would just take over."

Help also came from the other siblings in varying degrees. Bob, the history teacher, was always there in the evening to lend a hand with Buddy. Bob would exercise his arms and legs and they would talk, the conversation centered on whatever was happening that day in sports: how the Eagles were playing, how the teams at Tennent and elsewhere in the Suburban One looked. Linda, the nurse, would stop by to assist with some of the issues that came up with Buddy, including the care of his bedsores and the changing of his catheter. Joanne and Rose were somewhat less involved daily. While they would always assist when they were around, they had gone off on their own, Joanne to Doylestown and Rose to Philadelphia. Both had become secretaries. "The Nurse Nancy in me did not come out," Joanne says. "My mother called me once and said, 'I need your help with something.' And then said, 'Oh, I called the wrong one.'"

Some hard feelings emerged.

Joanne and Rose could feel it.

Occasionally, someone would say offhandedly, "You could do more." But it was not what was said but what was left unsaid: some underlying tension, perhaps even, as Rose remembers, some resentment. Even Buddy seemed to "keep score" of who did what as a barometer of who truly cared. Rose says, "There were no arguments, just a coolness that surrounded the subject."

But whatever unspoken grievances existed were just one aspect of the household dynamic that emerged. With her hands so full and the days so long, Rosemarie was no longer as accessible as she once was, either to her husband or to her other children. When one of her daughters would ask her out to lunch or to go shopping, Rosemarie would say, "I have to be back in a half hour for Buddy." Other than an occasional vacation, she and Bert were seldom able to get away. When she did get away, even if just for a short stay at the Jersey shore, she would worry how Buddy was doing without her, if the relatives who had come over to care for him were having any problems. She would think, *What if he needs something in the middle of the night?* Candidly Joanne remembers, "The day Buddy was hurt was the day my father lost his wife, and the other children lost their mother."

No one pondered that more than Buddy, who developed a keen appreciation for the burden that caring for him had become. Rosemarie assured him otherwise, begged him not to think of it that way, but sadness would envelope him when he weighed the consequences that his injury had had on others. When he had summarily told Karen to go on to Florida, he did so because he did not want to deny her the enjoyment of the good things that someone else could offer her. The same stirrings of conscience welled up in him whenever he considered the place he now had in the lives of his parents—both of them—and Bob, Joanne, Rose, Patti, and Linda.

And Jimmy.

Even as a boy, Jimmy was driven by one animating desire: to get Buddy to laugh. He became skilled at it. He and his siblings came up with a game called Orange. It was a silly diversion, yet enormous fun: Whenever Buddy said the word *orange,* Jimmy had to stop wherever he was and do exactly what Buddy told him. Jimmy remembers that Buddy used to "laugh his ass off" whenever they played it.

"Orange!" Buddy would shout, and order Jimmy, "Stand on your head!"

And Jimmy would stand on his head.

"Orange!" Buddy would order, "Bang your head against the wall."

And Jimmy would bang his head against the wall.

"Orange!" Buddy would order, "Come over here and let me slap you."

And Jimmy would kneel down by the bed as Buddy used what small strength remained in his biceps to elevate his hand and let it drop. The hand always hit Jimmy in the head—ouch! And the boys would squeal in amusement.

Hearing Buddy laugh gave Jimmy a sense of purpose. Even if he could not help Buddy to use his arms or legs again, he could provide him with a few seconds of relief, something that would allow Buddy to climb out from under the gray shroud that had settled over him. While it would be years before he would understand it fully, Jimmy formed an attachment to Buddy that he could not bring himself to separate from, not even when he had an opportunity to sign a professional baseball contract. He would discover that he and Buddy did not share the same dream, of one day leaving home to go off and play ball. Good Lord, Buddy would have moved heaven and earth to do that, if only just to see how far his ability could carry him. But Jimmy did not look at it that way. Baseball was something to have fun with— the way girls were something to have fun with. Twice given a chance to sign, he would just say he was not yet ready, that he still had some growing up to do. Somehow, it would always feel "too soon" to him . . . until it became too late.

No one was more excited than Buddy when Jimmy finally signed as a catcher with the Dodgers, the third team that had offered him a contract. Even Jimmy understood that there would not be a fourth.

Close to two years had passed since Jimmy had graduated from Tennent, but Buddy seemed to think it was good thing that he had not signed earlier, that a year of community college had given his brother a chance to grow up. On the March day in 1982 that Jimmy would leave for spring training in Vero Beach, Florida, Buddy told him, "Go down there and act like a pro. Be a man." From his wheelchair, Buddy looked out his window at the driveway. Jimmy tossed his bags in the trunk of the car, glanced over his shoulder, and waved good-bye.

. . . . .

Jimmy Miley in a play at the plate at William Tennent High School.
Sliding in safely is Steve Bono, future NFL quarterback.

. . . . .

TEN

Nice Wristbands

Sunshine poured from the heavens that day Roger Maris showed up at the Payson Complex in St. Petersburg, Florida. With the exception of a few extra pounds that had settled above his belt buckle, he looked the same as he did in 1961, the year he swatted sixty-one home runs for the New York Yankees and eclipsed the single-season record held by Babe Ruth. Even now he sported the same crew cut he wore on those old bubble-gum cards. The proprietor of a Budweiser distributorship that St. Louis Cardinals owner Gussie Busch had set him up with at the end of his career, Roger had come down from Gainesville to look in on his oldest son, Kevin, then an aspiring infielder in the Cardinals organization. Seeing Roger that day, it would have been hard to imagine that a year later he would be diagnosed with cancer, and in three more he would be lying under a profusion of red flowers at the Holy Cross Cemetery in Fargo, North Dakota. He was fifty-one when he passed away.

Out on the field at the end of their workout, Gary LaRocque summoned his players into a group. But Jimmy was only half-listening as the manager spoke, instead thinking of how in another hour he would be splayed on a towel at the edge of the Gulf of Mexico, a drowsy eye on the parade of bikinis that strolled up and down the beach. With his clipboard in hand, LaRocque began going over the schedule for the following day when he glanced across the diamond and spotted Maris, engaged in a casual conversation by the dugout. As a boy in the 1960s, LaRocque used to sit in the bleachers at old Yankee Stadium and worship in the glow of Maris and the legendary Mickey Mantle. The M&M Boys, they were called.

LaRocque paused and asked his players, "Does anyone know who that is over there?"

Jimmy looked over.

Crew cut . . . Marine . . .

Marine . . . Gomer Pyle . . .

Gomer Pyle . . .

Jimmy piped up, "Sergeant Carter?"

The other players snickered.

LaRocque narrowed his eyes and replied, "You better hope you have even an ounce of the talent that man had."

When Buddy later told this story to his brother-in-law Rudy Rudolf, Buddy said with a rueful chuckle, "The kid just doesn't get it." Rudy just shrugged and said, "That's Jimmy." Going back years, it seemed as if Jimmy had always been that way, especially in the face of authority. Anxiety would overtake him and he would begin to giggle. Or he would come up with some wisecrack out of the blue, which would generally leave people scratching their heads and asking themselves, *What did he just say?* But Jimmy was not a troublemaker or even disrespectful. In fact, he was eager to please, just not always sure how to do it. The teachers he had through school always liked him, but as Chick Donnelly, his basketball coach at Tennent would remember, he was an *"If only* kid . . . if only he would do this, if only he would do that." While as a teenager he had the strapping body of an adult, he had the wandering attention span of that same young boy who, upon hearing his friend tap on his bedroom window in his basement lair, would slip out the back door and join him behind the bushes for a cigarette.

"Jimmy," they'd say. "Oh, boy, what a knucklehead!" They'd remember a snowy evening when he was fourteen or fifteen. Jimmy, Donnie Schultz, and some others were out throwing snowballs at the cars sailing up Valley Road. They'd launch them and escape up a side street. But when a patrol car turned onto the block, Jimmy did not run, thinking, *No one saw me do anything.* Two girls were with him. Jimmy walked up with them to the cruiser and said, "Hey, how you doin'?" The cop said they had a report that he was throwing snowballs. Oh, no, Jimmy replied. But the cop said, "How come your hands are covered with ice?" From around the corner of a house up the street, Donnie looked on in horror as the cop snapped handcuffs on Jimmy and the girls and guided them into the backseat of the car. They then rode to the station, where an irate Rosemarie lashed into the arresting officer, "Why did you have to put handcuffs on him?" When she later spotted Schultz and the others walking by her house, Rosemarie leaned out the door and shouted, "Thanks a lot! You cost me seventy-five dollars for a ticket!"

Donnie asked Jimmy, "Why did you just stand there? You should have run."

Jimmy shrugged. "I figured he would let me go."

Jimmy laughs and says, "Mom was pissed at me. Somebody was always pissed."

Coaches, too—except they were dazzled by the wealth of ability he had. He just seemed to come to whatever sport he played naturally, as if it were ordained by his DNA. Give him a tennis racquet and chances were he'd whip you in straight sets, despite the fact that he'd never before played. In some ways he reminded his coaches of Buddy, who along with surpassing athletic skill had that same innate self-assuredness, that cocky air that used to drive Bert crazy whenever he spotted it. Jimmy had that. Walking out on the playing field seemed to transform him, caused him to become larger in the eyes of others—and perhaps even in his own. But what Donnelly remembers is that Jimmy wanted to be two athletes, not just one: the player Buddy could never be, and the one that his own size, strength, and speed promised that he had a chance to be. Somehow, Donnelly conjectured, Jimmy wanted to "roll the two of them into one and become this super athlete," even if he lacked the X factor that separates the few from the many. He even played football his senior year of high school, as if by doing so he could settle some of the old business that Buddy left unfinished.

"Oh, Jimmy!" Rosemarie exclaimed when she was told of his plan to play football. Players had to get the approval of their parents before they could play, and Rosemarie had some understandably grave concerns. But Buddy was on board with the idea, reassuring his mom (and Jimmy), "God would not let this happen twice to the same family." To placate her, Jimmy told her that he would only go out for the team as a punter, one of the positions he had played in the youth leagues. "How dangerous can that be?" Jimmy said. But Bert was not buying it, telling Rosemarie, "You know he's not going out just to be the kicker." Unenthusiastically, Rosemarie signed the release, only to discover later that Jimmy also planned to play not one but two other positions: wide receiver and defensive end. To protect himself, he wore two neck braces. Juzwiak says, "I think he was very conscious of Buddy. And I think we were worried about him. What would happen if another Miley kid went down?"

What had happened to Buddy had not been forgotten seven years later. With the first-string quarterback, Tom O'Neill, side-

lined with an injury, backup Steve Perlstein started the second game
of the season against Council Rock, only to go down just before the
half with what was feared to be a broken neck. Seeing Perlstein lying
there so still and then being driven away in an ambulance had a chilling effect on Jimmy and his teammates. Told that he would be going
in to play the second half, Carl Fisher, the third-string quarterback,
sat in the locker room at halftime with tears in his eyes. Jimmy looked
at him uneasily and said, "Come on, stop crying." But by the end of
that 30–0 loss, Jimmy sat at the end of the bench and began to cry
himself, thinking, *This is just not worth it.* He quit the team. But
Buddy told him to get back in there—and he did. With his parents,
Bob, and occasional other siblings in the stands to cheer him on,
Jimmy played better that year than Juzwiak or even Jimmy himself
had expected; the thirty receptions he had were good for 580 yards
and seven touchdowns. When he won All–Suburban One honors,
Juzwiak called his play "spectacular" and added, "I just hope football
gave something to Jim. Because it certainly took away from Buddy."

Good enough that senior year in football to attract attention
from the University of Arizona, Jimmy instead focused on baseball
that spring. Scouts had been following him since his sophomore year.
They'd give their cards to the Tennent head coach, Jeff Garrison, then
sit in groups of three or so in lawn chairs behind home plate. That
year, Norristown High School had an exceptionally skilled catcher,
Steve Bono, who would years later become a quarterback for the
San Francisco 49ers. But Garrison would always claim that Jimmy
was better than Bono. While Jimmy could be overzealous on the
field, even given to occasional incoherent outbursts that would leave
Garrison just shrugging his shoulders at the opposing coach as if to
say, "See what I have to deal with?" he offset that immaturity with an
array of physical tools. Line drives popped off his bat. From a squat-
ting position behind home plate, he became adept at picking runners

off base. And he had exceptional speed for a catcher. Invited to a
Baltimore tryout camp at old Memorial Stadium by scout Bob Carter
just before the 1980 June draft, Jimmy clocked a 6.8 from home plate
to second. Bob drove Jimmy down that day and remembers, "We had
always assumed that the Orioles would take him in the draft."

But the Orioles passed him over, choosing instead two catchers
in the early rounds: Al Pardo, in the second round with the overall
52nd selection and Carl Nichols, in the fourth round with the 103rd
overall selection. (Both ended up playing briefly for the Orioles.) Not
until later did the Houston Astros call the house with what proved to
be erroneous information: that Jimmy had been chosen by them in
the fifth round. In fact, he had been drafted in the tenth round with
250th overall pick. In any event, Bert was ecstatic that his youngest
boy had been chosen. Some friends had dropped by that evening for a
visit, and when one of them asked Jimmy, "So, are you going to sign?"
Bert interjected, "Oh, he's going to sign!" Irritated, Jimmy slipped
away to the basement and buried his face in his pillow, thinking of
Andrea, the girlfriend he would have to leave behind . . . and Buddy.
It would be hard to leave him, unfair. Buddy told him, "Go ahead!
Go down and enjoy yourself!" Offered $5,000 by the Astros, Jimmy
told them no, that he would go on and play at Montgomery County
Community College. Livid, Bert sequestered himself in his bedroom
and sulked for a week.

What Jimmy told himself was that he could do better than the
tenth round, that a year or so of playing in college would enhance his
standing. Consequently, he also gave the Cleveland Indians a wide
berth when they selected him with the thirty-sixth overall pick in
the second round of the 1981 January Draft–Second Phase, which
consisted of the pool of players from the previous spring who had
gone unsigned. The perplexed Cleveland scout who dropped by the
house told him, "Everybody usually signs." But by then the offer he

was looking at had gone down to $2,000, which he told a reporter was "hardly gas money." So he played that spring at Montgomery County Community College—and he played well—but dropped out at the end of the year due to poor grades. By the beginning of what would have been his sophomore year, he got a job doing temporary labor for the Manpower Program. But in November he got a call from Carter, who had left the Orioles organization to work for the Los Angeles Dodgers. Carter told him if he could still run a 6.8, he would sign him. Jimmy drove out to Chambersburg on his twentieth birthday and did just that. The Dodgers gave him $1,000 to sign and a date to report to Vero Beach, Florida, the following March. Carter told his boss, Dodgers scouting director Ben Wade, "Ben, I think we got a good one."

Uniformed deities walked the earth at Dodgertown, the by-now graying figures of *Boys of Summer* lore. On any given day, a young player could look up and see Duke Snider or Pee Wee Reese standing there, or perhaps some Dodger of later vintage, the legendary Sandy Koufax or Don Drysdale. They came down each year to lend a hand with spring training—and reconnect. Left paralyzed years before by a car wreck, Roy Campanella worked with the young catchers from his wheelchair, giving them instruction in the way the Dodger catchers were expected to carry themselves behind the plate. "Campy" passed it along just it had been passed to him by Branch Rickey, the visionary who shattered the color line in baseball by signing Jackie Robinson and who founded Dodgertown as a "baseball college" in 1948. When Jimmy reported on March 17, 1982, the place had evolved into a setting that joined state-of-the-art instruction with the air of a pampering spa. Cookouts were held by owner Peter O'Malley at the swimming pool, one of which LaRocque remembered had a Christmas theme that included a shipment of snow. By design, the big club dressed in a locker room that adjoined quarters occupied by the minor leaguers, and there Jimmy encountered All-Star first baseman Steve Garvey, who flashed him that Sunset Strip smile and said, "Nice wristbands."

Pro ball was a structured world that Jimmy was not prepared for. From the beginning, the Dodgers had slotted him to leave on April 1 for extended spring training in St. Petersburg. There, he would play on a squad of Dodger farmhands who would be shipped later in the spring to one of their Rookie League or Class A affiliates. LaRocque would lead them through drills in the morning, and at 11:00 A.M. or so, before the Florida sun grew unbearably hot, they would have a game with one of the other clubs that had players based at the Payson Complex. With the additional workouts that typically followed, it could easily be a ten-hour day. LaRocque says that it was not uncommon for players to experience trouble adapting to what was expected of them, given that some had never been away from home before or off on their own. One player with Jimmy that spring who did adjust was Mariano Duncan, an undrafted free agent from the Dominican Republic who would play twelve seasons in the major leagues. But Jimmy would do "stuff" that exposed his inability to approach the sport as a job.

One day he walked out on the field wearing his old helmet from the Warrington Athletic Association. Go back in and get your helmet, LaRocque told him.

On another he asked if could leave in the second inning to pick up his girlfriend, Andrea, at the airport. Quizzically, LaRocque looked at him, shrugged, and said, "Go on."

On still another he scraped the bridge of his nose in a collision during a rundown play. LaRocque told him to go in for treatment but Jimmy told him, "No, I can play." LaRocque gave him a hard look and insisted, "Get in and see the trainer!"

But Jimmy would share only good news with Buddy. They spoke

once or twice a week. Jimmy would use the pay phone outside the one-bedroom apartment he shared with three teammates from California. Instead of collecting his coins the way one of his roommates did to phone his girlfriend back home, Jimmy dialed the operator and charged his calls to a number he had for a local bank. Given his illicit billing scheme, Jimmy would keep his calls to Buddy short, just long enough to pass along some highlights. When they played the Red Sox affiliate, Jimmy got three hits off Mark "the Bird" Fidrych, the eccentric former Tigers phenom who was working his way back that spring from arm trouble. Fidrych stopped in the bar later, spotted Jimmy, and said, "Good going today. Three for four! Man, you should be proud of yourself." Told of this encounter, Buddy laughed, just as he had when Jimmy had shared with him the Roger Maris story or how back at Dodgertown he found himself splashing in the same swimming pool with O'Malley. "Jeez, Jimmy!" Buddy told him, his laughter yielding to concern. "What are you doing swimming with the owner?" For Jimmy, it was always good to talk to Buddy again—it seemed to lift them both—yet he would always feel sad when he got off the phone. Some part of him would wonder, *Why am I down here getting paid to play baseball when the real work is back at home?*

Only years later would he begin to piece together what had happened that spring with the Dodgers, how easily opportunities can be given and withdrawn. As the weeks passed in Florida, he told himself that he was holding his own, even if he was only batting .250. But when he had a chance to think it over, he would come to understand that his head had not been in the game the way it should have been. It was back home with Buddy, or with Andrea, or down at the beach, where he would hang out instead of attending the optional workouts LaRocque held. Or it was off with pals, who one evening spilled from a bar with their bellies full of beer and looked on with amusement as Jimmy announced, "Watch this!" Jimmy jumped over the hood of a parked car. Everyone laughed. Everyone always did. Someone later told him that one of the coaches drove by and saw him do that.

But he did not see the end coming, even if the signs were there in bold relief. The day before, he charged down to second base on a single to right, only to be tagged out when he overran the bag and the right fielder threw behind him. While it had not been a heads-up play, Jimmy was not thinking of it when one of the coaches tapped him on the shoulder the following day and told him that LaRocque wanted to see him in his office. The Dodgers had Class A teams at Vero Beach and out in California at Lodi, so Jimmy was expecting LaRocque to hand him his assignment. As he strolled through the clubhouse, his teammates shouted, "Lodi! Lodi! Lodi!" The manager was seated at his desk when Jimmy came in and closed the door behind him.

LaRocque looked up at him. "Jim, we've signed another catcher."

LaRocque began to say more, but Jimmy interrupted and asked, "When does my plane leave?"

Jimmy was out the door before LaRocque finished saying, "Tomorrow."

One by one, his ex-teammates came up to Jimmy as he cleaned out his locker. Some of them had tears in their eyes. Jimmy went back to his apartment and called home from the phone booth outside, again charging the call to the local bank. He had hoped that anyone but his father would pick up. Sure enough, Bert answered. "Dad . . . ," Jimmy said, not knowing where to begin. "I got released." There was a silence on the other end. "Okay," Bert said, "come on home." Jimmy went out that evening to drink beer and shoot some pool with his roommates, who consoled him by saying, "Man, they released *you*!" It would be the last time he would see any of them. They would go off to their lives and he would go off to his. When the bar closed, he walked outside and up the street and before long found himself standing under a billboard at the entrance of the Payson Complex that announced HOME OF THE METS. Jimmy picked up a rock and threw it. It bounced off the sign and fell to the ground.

FUND-RAISERS . . .

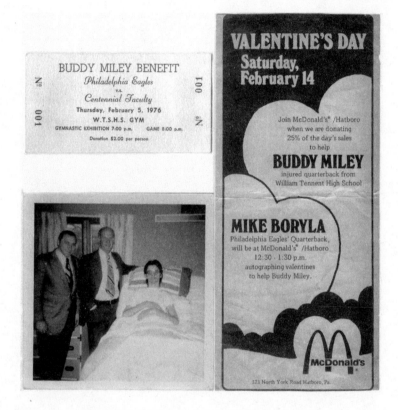

Buddy with Alan Ameche (left) and Tom Landry (right).

ELEVEN

Game Face

When they were still just teenagers in Kenosha, Wisconsin, Lino Ameche would help Yvonne Molinaro up onto the handle bars of his bicycle and pedal her to the hospital, where her father was dying of cancer. They were fourteen. Classmates then at Washington Junior High School, she remembers a conversation they once had. "If I were you," she told him, "I would think about changing my name." *Lino* reminded her of a jingle for a popular cleaning solution. Grinning, he looked at her and replied, "If I were you, I would get my teeth fixed." So she did—and he did: Yvonne got braces, and Lino went down to the courthouse and for fifty cents officially changed his given name to Alan, perhaps because Yvonne had a starry eye for screen heartthrob Alan Ladd. But it would be Alan Ameche who would sweep her up in his arms and carry her across the threshold.

A Heisman Trophy winner at the University of Wisconsin in 1954, Alan "the Horse" Ameche would come to be remembered as the Baltimore Colts fullback who poured into the end zone with the

winning touchdown in what would be memorialized as "the Great-
est Game Ever Played," the 21–17 overtime victory by the Colts over
the New York Giants in the NFL Championship Game at Yankee
Stadium in December 1958. But Yvonne remembers her husband as a
man of some dimension, not just a splendid athlete and astute entre-
preneur who partnered with former Colts teammate Gino Marchetti
to create Gino's, a popular hamburger chain that was ultimately sold
for millions. Away from his varied professional obligations, Ameche
was an enthusiastic patron of the arts, especially classical music. The
symphonies of Beethoven flowed though the rooms of his Main Line
estate. While Yvonne says he was "very Italian and had a very short
fuse," she also remembers him as a caring soul who gave of himself in
quiet yet consequential ways in his work with the Fellowship of Christian Athletes. No one would come to know that better than Buddy
Miley.

Upon hearing of a young quadriplegic man in Warminster,
Ameche drove out to see Buddy, perhaps a year or so after the injury.
They sat and talked. Quickly, Ameche became fond of him. Buddy
had that skill with people—that charm. In the years that followed,
Ameche exhibited what Yvonne would call his "ability to go the extra
mile." Sensing the pressure that weighed on Bert and Rosemarie, he
arranged to send them on a Caribbean vacation. Unexpectedly, a
travel agent who worked with Ameche called Rosemarie one day and
asked, "How would you like to go to Antigua?" It was a relief to get
away, yet Rosemarie felt out of place in the evening among women
who wore long gowns and diamonds. But she would forever feel in-
debted to Ameche, if only because of the interest he showed in Buddy.
One day he asked Yvonne to join the two of them for lunch. But an
uneasy feeling came over her as she sat across the table from Buddy.

"I was just uncomfortable," Yvonne says. "It was out of my comfort level to see someone so badly damaged by a game that had given us so much."

What happened to Buddy is written in the fine print of the tacit agreement every player signs off on whenever he dons a football uniform. Ameche understood that, as did the coaches and players who dropped by to see Buddy in his hospital room or at his house. The Eagles' owner, Leonard Tose, the wizened trucking tycoon whose giving spirit extended to the blackjack tables in Atlantic City and the assorted cocktail waitresses who appeared at his side, sent quarterback Roman Gabriel, and tight end/linebacker Marlin McKeever, in his helicopter to see Buddy at Sacred Heart Hospital. The Eagles' general manager, Jim Murray, a pious soul who joined with Tose to help in the founding of the Ronald McDonald House, arranged for other players to give Buddy what he called a "a hug on the phone," including the Dallas Cowboys' quarterback, Roger Staubach. The rotund Murray told them, "This is an all-American great kid." A photograph even came in from Broadway Joe, who inscribed it: "To my o-o-o-old pal Buddy Miley. From Joe Namath." On a Sunday when his team was playing the Eagles, Cowboys coach Tom Landry showed up at the door at 7:30 A.M. Buddy could not believe his ears when Rosemarie stepped into his room and announced, "Guess who's here?" Landry removed his fedora and for well over an hour engaged Buddy in football talk. But something unspoken passed between them that day, just as it had with Ameche, Gabriel, and any of the others who had or would come by: that Buddy belonged to an eternal brotherhood. And it could have been any of them lying in that bed but for the grace of God.

Buddy remained in the public eye. The local papers followed him—and Jimmy, when he began to come into his own as an athlete. Reporters checked in with Buddy as the years passed, in part because

it was becoming increasingly clear that America had untold other
Buddy Mileys—your neighbor four doors down, perhaps, or the
son of that woman you saw occasionally at the grocery store. Until
Temple University orthopedic surgeon Dr. Joseph Torg came along,
these were the uncounted casualties of football, young men whose
bodies had become useless due to cervical spine injuries. Some fifteen
miles from where Buddy lay in bed, Torg began counting them as
part of his National Football Head and Neck Injury Registry. What
Torg uncovered was a revelation, one that led to rule changes to en-
sure safer conduct on the playing field, the rethinking of how coaches
instructed players to tackle, and ultimately a decline in catastrophic
events.

As an old expression reminds us, science advances on the shoulders of giants. Torg, a caustic man with an affinity for speaking his
mind, was every inch a giant in the embryonic era of sports medicine.
In looking back on that period, Dr. Guy W. Fried, the chief medical
officer at the Magee Rehabilitation center in Philadelphia, characterized it as a "dark time" given what we would come to know. Thirty-
four years ago, MRI and CAT scans were not yet in use, and we
lacked of knowledge in how to spot and treat players who had a potential spinal-cord injury. Chances are that even five years later
Buddy would have received far better emergency care on the field,
and he would surely not have been placed in an ambulance with a
player who had a broken leg. But not until Torg shed a light on what
had become a hidden crisis did anyone begin paying attention. According to the data he collected for his National Football Head and
Neck Injury Registry, the five-year period from 1971 to 1975 saw
seventy-seven young players die of severe neck injuries, and another
ninety-nine suffer from cervical fracture-dislocations that led to
permanent quadriplegia. In a scathing interview that appeared in
Sports Illustrated, Torg scolded society for allowing these tragedies

to be "slipped under the rug" and assailed the football world for pro-
moting "the use of the head in blocking, tackling, and running with
the ball." Torg said, "God gave us heads for thinking, not to be used
as instruments of war." Of the coaches and others who presided over
this carnage, he added, "The people responsible for the conduct of
the game have the collective mentality of a herd of field oxen."

Torg was saying that these were not "freak accidents," as they
were often shrugged off as in an effort to store the event in some understandable place. Instead, they were the by-product of using the
head as a battering ram, of dangerous conditioning exercises such as
the one Buddy had performed with the Little Quakers, injuring himself, the aptly termed "nutcracker drill." Coaches and indeed the players themselves during that unenlightened era overestimated the safety
that helmets provided and used the head accordingly. Says Torg, "I
remember vividly when plastic helmets came out in 1951, there was a
great emphasis on sticking it to the other player, spearing them and
hitting them with your head." In fact, some contraptions were even
developed to aid in the development of that technique, such as the
spring-loaded Tacklematic Hitting Machine, which accounted for
more than a few catastrophic injuries. Torg unveiled the hazards of it
in an article in *The Journal of the American Medical Association* and
drove the company that produced it into extinction. While incidents
would decline in the years to come due to the heightened awareness
that had driven the NFL, NCAA, and the National High School
Athletic Association to penalize spearing, the subject continued to
draw attention as some celebrated players ended up as quadriplegics. Two of them would help frame the debate for years to come:
New England Patriots wide receiver Daryl Stingley, upended in a
1978 exhibition game by the lethal Oakland Raiders free-safety back
Jack Tatum (who would author *They Call Me Assassin*); and The
Citadel linebacker Marc Buoniconti, injured while tackling an East

Tennessee opponent in 1985 and who would found the Miami Project to Cure Paralysis.

Whatever else he had come away from football with, Buddy embraced the concept that coaches have been hammering at players for years: Keep your head down, your ass up, and keep driving. In interviews he always had his game face on. When it came to the subject of a cure, he told himself and others that he would do just that—hang in there until someone came up with an advancement that could help him. One day he told his brother Bob, "Whatever it takes. Five years? I can lie here five years. Or ten. Or fifteen. Or even longer." Until that day came, Buddy said he would be a good soldier. Updates on progress toward a cure came from the Spinal Cord Society, and it gave him the glimmer of hope that his doctors were not prepared to provide. Torg examined him and concluded, "He had an irreversible injury." Other opinions echoed that. Little Quakers founder Bob Levy arranged for Buddy to be seen at the Hospital of the University of Pennsylvania by Dr. Frederick Murtaugh, who operated on him to relieve the pressure on his spinal cord. Candidly, Murtaugh told Buddy beforehand that the odds were 100–1 against his experiencing any improvement and that he could end up losing the small function that he had. Ultimately, the surgery had no effect either way.

Even if they were beyond probability, the goals Buddy set for his recovery provided him with some buoyancy. In his conversations with Karen years before at the hospital, he had spoken of playing baseball in the spring, which had not seemed to either of them to be unreasonable. Neither of them had a firm grasp then of the extent of the injury Buddy had, only that bones break and eventually heal. But Dr. Fried explains that the bone was not the issue. "Bones are stupid," says Fried, who adds that it is not uncommon for young patients to think "they can just shake it off." "You have broken one. Indeed, you have broken your neck. There is a bone in there. A seventeen-year-old knows many people who have had broken bones. But it is not the broken bone that is the problem. The bones are only this hard encasement the sole purpose of which is to protect the spinal cord, which is this live electrical tissue that is extremely fragile and extremely sensitive that is an extension of your brain and goes into your arms and legs. So it is a bone like no other, closer to being a skull. What you have to understand is that you have not just broken a bone but your central nervous system, the communication between your head and your body. Of course, it is not intuitive to understand this, that you can separate your head from your body." Consequently, it did not surprise Fried that Buddy would have told a local reporter in November 1974 that he was "shooting for June" to regain the use of his upper body and hands.

"This is a young man who is on top of his game," says Fried. "Being a young man, nothing bad can possibly happen. Chances are he had never heard of anyone having had a spinal-cord injury or realized that that was even a possibility."

Uncoupling himself from the place in the world he once occupied seemed on some days to be beyond Buddy. In the sanctuary of sleep he was still seventeen, always walking or running somewhere, perhaps holding hands on a date or just spreading peanut butter and jelly on a piece of bread. But with the beginning of each new day, the dream would slip away and he would be back in bed with the covers over his still body. Going out with the aid of Bob or Jimmy or someone else, he became conscious of the way people looked at him, the sideways looks they gave him as his wheelchair moved through a crowd. Perhaps he had spotted it in Yvonne when Ameche had introduced them, that vague uneasiness that seemed to come over people whenever they encountered him. Even his old friends seemed unsure of how to act or what to say. Guy Driesbach, who had thrown up upon seeing him at Sacred Heart Hospital, avoided Buddy for a year before Buddy called him and said, "Are you going to come visit me or what?" Driesbach stammered and replied, "I can't. I can't come to see you, Bud." But his friend did and found what Dave Heilbrun, Brian Sheehan, and others would discover: When you dropped by to see Buddy, you were going to be there awhile, as he peppered you with questions on how your life was going. Hearing how other people were doing connected him to the world beyond his window and indeed gave him purpose. Friends unburdened themselves to him and would always leave feeling better, if not to some degree silly once they looked at themselves through the prism of his injury. Invariably, they would think, *What problems could I have that could possibly compare to what he has to face every day?* Always, it seemed to them that they had gotten more out of the visit than he did.

He became someone they could turn to.

And they did.

Eucharistic minister Joanne Johnston began serving him Communion each Sunday. "I remember he said once, 'Joanne, something is bothering you. What is it?'" she says. "He was so perceptive that way. At that time, my mother had not been doing too well. Of course, I did not want to bring my sorrows to him. But Buddy wanted you to share them with him. He was an incredible listener."

Carmen Frangiosa stopped by the house to see him. Buddy did not blame him for what happened, not for a second. But Frangiosa still carried with him a degree of guilt, even if he was not sure what he could have done to avert what had happened. He continued to play football and accepted a scholarship at Wake Forest, where he was a starting guard and played with his old P-W teammate Steve Bernardo. As he sat by the bed during a visit when he was still in college, Frangiosa remembered that fall day in 1973 and pictured Buddy, how he jabbed his finger in the air at him and his teammates and told them they were overrated. Even though only a few years had elapsed at that point, it seemed to Frangiosa as if an eternity had passed as Buddy looked at him from his bed and pumped him for information: "What is college like? What is game day like?" Frangiosa told him how his Wake Forest team had just traveled to Ann Arbor to play Michigan before over one hundred thousand fans. The Wolverines had beaten them, 31–0, but it was an experience Frangiosa told Buddy he would never forget.

"You walk down a runway and onto the field and you suddenly get hit by this wall of noise," Frangiosa said. "It sounds like thousands and thousands of bees buzzing."

"Is it harder than high school? Are the guys better?"

"Yeah. They're all good. Everyone is good. In high school, you'll play against two good guys. In college, they'll be eight good guys out there. They're quicker, stronger."

Buddy absorbed that. "How good were the quarterbacks?"

"They were good. We had a real good guy and Michigan had a real good guy."

"How do you think I would have done?"

Frangiosa smiled. "Hey, Buddy. You could have played."

"You think so?"

"Absolutely. You had the talent."

"You really believe that?"

Frangiosa told him, "Yeah."

But what Buddy had to do was reinvent himself, create a new normalcy that allowed him strike out on his own in some way. To that end, he entered a local rehabilitation hospital for physical therapy, only to encounter what he would later describe as coarse treatment. "I was there ten days and came out dehydrated," he told the *Bucks County Courier Times*. That was the extent of the formal rehabilitation he received, which left him unable to feed himself or learn how to drive, which someone with his level of injury could have done.

Moreover, he did not place himself in a position to become part of the evolving rehabilitation system. According to Mary Schmidt, the Magee Spinal Cord Injury program director, "The 1980s were a big boom in education and vocational opportunities." Buddy remained more or less housebound, cared for by Rosemarie and whoever happened to be there to pitch in. Occasionally, a physical therapist would come by the house to work with him, or Bob and Jimmy would exercise his legs or get him up in his brace and walk him.

Whatever else human beings require to survive, one fundamental ingredient is a sense of a definable future, the anticipation that things will somehow get better. Early on, Buddy optimistically spoke of picking up some college credits and perhaps one day owning a sporting-goods store. But the years passed and he had still not committed to some course of action until a sports agent he knew recommended that he line up speaking appearances for athletes. It was perfect for Buddy, or so it seemed. He would contact athletes that had grown up in the area who had gone on to play pro ball. Under a headline that announced this enterprise as his "first venture into the outside world," a local paper pictured him in a trimmed beard sitting behind an electric typewriter.

It was a good feeling, this sense that better days where ahead, even if the "rescue ship" bearing a cure that Fried speaks of was still somewhere far off, Even if Rosemarie would have to do the secretarial work for him—which she did, gladly—a world full of new possibilities opened up. Perhaps he would even go national with it at some point, hire a staff and spend Wednesdays on the golf course. He would get a place of his own, get out of the house finally and out from under the brooding presence of his father. On the cresting wave of this enthusiasm, he began thinking again of Karen and what had become of her. Nine years had passed since he had last seen her: New Year's Eve, 1974. She had come up from Florida to stay with a friend, had a car accident, and had gone back home without a word. Unable to locate a current telephone number for her in the Florida directories—her name had been misspelled in their high school yearbook—he prevailed upon a mutual friend for it and called her in May or June of 1982. When she picked up the phone, he immediately recognized her voice—how could he ever forget it? A recording device Buddy had hooked up to his phone captured the conversation. But only one end of it: his.

"It's been so damn long. God, I can't believe how long it's been."

"I'm holding up pretty good that way. . . . You're not getting old. You're twenty-five, right? And you'll be twenty-six October seventh . . . Oh, the sixth."

"I've got my own number. I'm a big businessman now. . . . No, I'm doing good. I'm doing really good. The big part is, I'm so damn lonely, you know? I always had like a crying heart. . . . Yeah, I know. . . ."

"Last time I called, I called your parents. I still had the number somehow. This was years ago, I guess while you were still engaged. And I talked to your brother. I'm sure he never left the message. But he said something about you were in Michigan. What were you doing in Michigan?"

"Why do you say that? Why do you say that? Karen! You've still got that cute laugh. . . . I've missed you an unbelievable amount. I really have. I think of you every day. I swear to God. I swear. Every day. . . . We had something very special."

"So you look the same, huh? You look the same? . . . Huh? I'm not crazy. . . . You are. You are sexy."

"You never come up here? . . . Are you serious? . . . Uh-huh. . . . Come up, I'm moving into my own place. . . . Uh-huh. . . . Bring your daughter up."

"Have you? I've been waiting, too. . . . Uh-huh. . . . I love you. I probably shouldn't say that, but that's my true feeling. I always have.

I always will. I'm telling you, one day. . . . I get this newsletter once a month from the Spinal Cord Society. I'm serious. . . . I'm going to go to France and get a miracle and the hell with modern science. I'm going to get on my feet."

"I think I look pretty good. I have a mustache right now. During the winter, I have a full beard. My hair looks good. My sister's a hairstylist. Yeah, Patti."

"I know it is. . . . Does she?"

"Oh, Karen, your voice. I love it."

. . . . .

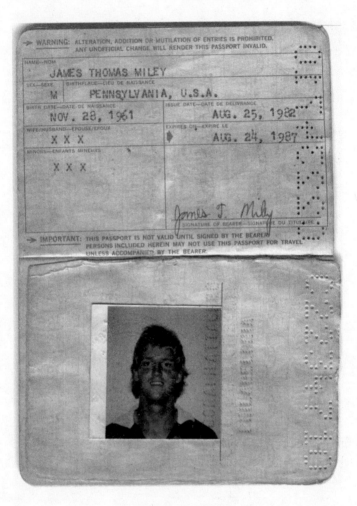

Off to Lourdes . . .

TWELVE

A Bunch of Buddys

Jimmy would remember thinking, *What is everybody looking at?* As they walked through the airport in Paris and later through the streets of Lourdes—Buddy in his wheelchair, Jimmy behind it, pushing it through the tangle of pedestrians—it occurred to him how very far they were from home. It seemed like ages ago that they were back in Warminster, the two of them preparing for this big adventure that would carry them from JFK Airport, across the Atlantic Ocean, and to the Sanctuary of Our Lady of Lourdes, where legions of incurables have come in search of divine healing. Other than the cup of orange juice Jimmy spilled on Buddy, it had been an uneventful trip, albeit both of them were now tired and hungry. Jimmy had eaten some passable lasagna on the plane, and Buddy a beef-and-bean dish so inedible that he had to spit it out.

As they sat in their room at the Imperial Hotel, Jimmy flipped on the tape recorder he had carried along with him. They were always fooling around with recording stuff in those days; Jimmy used to drive around back home and describe whatever he happened to see, just so Buddy could get a feel for what was going on out in the world. Jimmy began the chronicle of their journey to France as soon as they had landed at Charles de Gaulle Airport: The rain has stopped and the sun is beginning to break through . . . the Frenchwomen are not "too enthusiastic about us . . . I think we'd do better in Warminster" . . . and the room at the hotel has "a puny bed and no pillows." Inside that room, they laugh over how they just got stuck in the elevator.

JIMMY: What is it? Eight P.M.?

BUDDY: Close.

JIMMY: Yeah, I'm having peanut-butter bread for dinner. Buddy's having peanut-butter bread with a little jam. We have about ten pieces of bread left.

BUDDY: Thanks, Mom, for getting jam.

JIMMY: Yeah, you got us jam instead of jelly.

BUDDY: I sent Jimmy out on the town and he was out buying the groceries, a bottle of Coke and a bottle of orange soda.

JIMMY: I'm going to drink my warm Coke that cost seven and a half francs. Nobody ripped us off yet.

BUDDY: I'll have a sip of that.

JIMMY: This soda is like Alka-Seltzer.

BUDDY: Plop, plop, fizz, fizz. You drink the orange stuff.

JIMMY: We'll take you to Lourdes tomorrow.

BUDDY: We'll report back later.

JIMMY: *Bon voyage. Oui! Oui!*

A banner had been draped across the front of the house when Jimmy returned from Florida five months before: WELCOME HOME! Groggy from his evening of beer drinking with his former team-mates, Jimmy packed up the following day and was driven to the airport by one of the coaches, who had his girlfriend with him in the front seat. The woman seemed irritated, Jimmy sensed as he looked at the back of her head, as if it pissed her off that she had to spend part of her day off taking "some punk kid" to the airport. Seeing the sign on the house cheered him up, but he was even better seeing Buddy and the others again, even if his father just looked on in stony silence. But Bert no longer annoyed Jimmy as he once had, not since Jimmy had come home from a game a few years before and told him he had gone three for four at the plate—and Bert had asked why he had not gone four for four. Jimmy began to shrug off such asides as "the same old shit," just as Buddy had and even Bob. Nothing was ever good enough. Impassively, Bert looked on from the head of the table as Jimmy regaled everyone at dinner with the handful of Spanish words he had learned in Florida. Grinning, he said, *"Baseball* is *beisbol.* And *dammit* is *caramba."* Outwardly, he seemed unshaken by how his career had gone so off course, yet deep down he could not help but feel he had disappointed everyone.

Summer unfolded at a leisurely pace. With Buddy upstairs in his bed by the window, Jimmy moved back down in the basement, which he would come to call "the dungeon." During the day, he drove a delivery van for Delcrest Medical Services and Supplies and dropped off oxygen, walkers, wheelchairs, and such to customers. To stay in shape, he played baseball three or four evenings a week for Cedarbook in the Pen-Del League, where he hoped to attract the eye of a scout and get another opportunity to play pro ball. The Eagles' general manager, Jim Murray, had some baseball contacts and, as a favor to Buddy, had said that he would look into helping Jimmy get lined up somewhere. On the weekends, Jimmy would kick back and enjoy himself, drink beer with friends or go on dates. His high school girlfriend, Andrea, had gone off with someone else by then, but he had not had any intention of settling down. He was still only twenty, young enough to get his baseball career back on track. He told himself he would be better prepared when his chance came around again.

Until that happened, Jimmy was perfectly happy to be back home. Seeing Buddy again each day and helping out with his care gave him purpose, and Jimmy always enjoyed the repartee they shared. While Buddy had been disappointed that Jimmy had been cut by the Dodgers—at one point telling his neighbor George Bushman, "Can you believe he went down there and blew it?"—he could not help but be amused by some of the exploits his brother had related. Buddy would shake his head and dissolve into laughter over something Jimmy had done, and that always gave Jimmy a feeling of accomplishment. Of course, the two had disagreements, when Jimmy would dig his heels in over something and Buddy would shout, "Mom, get him out of here!" But calm would soon descend upon the house again, and Jimmy would reemerge from his basement hideaway and he and Buddy would have a laugh. From what Jimmy would remember, Buddy was in especially good spirits that summer, in part because he had that business he was starting and because Alan Ameche had told him he would underwrite a trip for him to Lourdes. In the parlance of the sport that had placed him in his predicament, Buddy looked upon it as the ultimate Hail Mary pass.

Miracles had abounded in the catechism books of his youth, none of which would have played larger in his consideration than John 5:1–18, in which Jesus heals a lame man by the pool of Bethesda: *Now a certain man was there who had an infirmity thirty-eight years. When Jesus saw him lying there and knew that he had already been in that condition a long time, He said to him, "Do you want to be made well?" The sick man answered Him, "Sir, I have no man to put me into the pool when the water is stirred up; but while I am coming, another steps down before me." Jesus said to him, "Rise, take up your bed, and walk." And immediately the man was made well, took up his bed, and walked.*

Biblical passages such as this gave Buddy hope, even if only the belief in some slender possibility for recovery that existed beyond what the doctors had told him. Oh, but how he had prayed for it to be so, that even if he could not get up and walk again, he would be relieved of the unendurable pain that he was in, which became harder and harder to cope with as the years passed! What he would have given for the electrical shocks to cease shooting through him!

No option would be left unexplored, even if it seemed beyond the realm of the orthodox. From the beginning, he welcomed spiritual intervention. When he had been at Sacred Heart Hospital, he found that he had no appetite, which caused his weight to drop and his mother to worry. But one day Ed Cherosky stopped in his room with one of the blood-soaked gloves that had belonged to Pio of Pietrelcina—or Padre Pio, as he became popularly known. The glove had been worn by the Capuchin priest and later Roman Catholic saint to cover up his stigmata. Blood flowed from penny-size holes in his hands and his feet in the approximate location of the crucifixion wounds of Jesus Christ. Of enduring belief in the healing powers that the glove possessed, Cherosky roamed the area hospitals with it. He had heard what had happened to Buddy and showed up with the glove, which he placed on Buddy in his bed. Incredibly—or so the story is told by Rosemarie—later that same day Buddy yelled out to the nursing staff, "What does a guy got to do to get some food around here?" Whenever Cherosky came back with the glove through the years, Buddy would say that he experienced "a warmth inside of him," a phenomenon that his friend Joanne Johnston said was "not a physical healing but gave him the strength to go on."

No one ever heard Buddy ask, "Why did this happen to me?" Yet he had to wonder why he had been asked to bear this cross, if some unknowable plan was behind his affliction. Early on, he recounted an odd scene to his sister Rose. Lying in his parents' bedroom when he'd just gotten home from the hospital, he looked up at the wall and saw a vision of a crucifix, upon which Christ unmoored his arm of the cross and pointed a finger at him. Concerned that people would think he was just hallucinating, or had perhaps even gone crazy, he asked Rose not to share this with anyone. Nor did he himself ever bring it up—not with his mother or any of his other siblings, and apparently not with the clergy who came to his house each Sunday and gave him Communion. The visiting priests and later Johnston would say in their blessing, "May God the Father bless you. . . . May God the Son heal you. . . . May God the Holy Spirit enlighten you. . . . May almighty God bless you, the Father, and the Son, and the Holy Spirit."

Given even the longest shot of walking again, Buddy would give it a look, always hopeful but never overly so. Within a few years of his injury, he attended an event at the George Washington Motor Lodge in Willow Grove, where thousands of people with assorted physical and other concerns showed up to hear televangelist Pat Robertson. With Buddy that day were his parents and Jimmy, who still was just thirteen or so and had been having problems with his throat. Breathing in cool air caused it to close up. Mesmerized, Jimmy remembers how Robertson strode across the stage, waded into the crowd, and shouted, "Someone has a money problem. That has been taken care of. . . . Someone has a hole in their heart. That has been taken care of. . . . Someone has a throat problem. That has been taken care of." Immediately, Jimmy held up his arms and exclaimed that Robertson was speaking of him. Sighing, his mother looked at him and said, "Stop that carrying on." But Jimmy says with a chuckle, "Believe it or not, I never had a problem with my throat again." And he remembers that Buddy told him, "You were always barging in on my miracles."

But eight or so years later Buddy would go to Lourdes, and Jimmy would take him. Jimmy was chosen because, as their mother would say, "We always said, 'If you have a job to do, give it to Jimmy, he'll do it.' " It was always said in jest, but it was true. Physically, Jimmy was big and strong enough to handle Buddy, who was not just heavy but unfolded into jutting angles of elbows and knees. But Jimmy had also developed considerable patience, which was especially useful whenever he and Buddy had to go somewhere. On their journey to France in October 1982, Jimmy carried Buddy on and off planes and on and off buses, careful to cradle him in his arms as he moved him in and out of his wheelchair. In the air and again at the hotel, he would feed Buddy, give him something to drink, and attend to his catheter bag. To begin that Saturday in Lourdes, he dressed Buddy and combed his hair. But before Jimmy did any of that, he turned on the tape recorder.

JIMMY: Day two. Held hostage.
BUDDY: Just getting up. Gonna go eat peanut butter and jelly
    for breakfast again. And get some Coke.
JIMMY: This town blows!

But Jimmy would not think that years later when he looked back on it. Steeped in vivid fall colors, Lourdes was picturesque, with a river curling through it and an old bridge that led to the shrine. It was near the end of the season, which runs from April to October, yet it was teeming with visitors—or, as they are called, pilgrims. Millions of ailing people have gone there each year since 1860, the place where two years before Bernadette Soubirous, a fourteen-year-old girl, had witnessed the apparition of a white-robed woman in a grotto called Massabielle. From February to July 1858, Bernadette had seen eighteen such apparitions. On the day of the sixteenth—March 25—she began digging until there was a small puddle, which grew into a pool, and then what has become the hallowed spring. Only a relative handful of people had been recognized by the Church as having been cured by immersing themselves in it—sixty-five, as of the fall of 1982—and yet as Jimmy wheeled Buddy into the grotto, both of them were overcome by the powerful imagery of the scene before them: Hanging from the walls were discarded canes, crutches, and wheelchairs.

Jimmy handed off Buddy to an attendant, who guided his wheelchair behind a curtain. Jimmy stood outside.

Buddy could be heard: "No, get Jimmy! Get my brother!"

The attendant slid back the curtain and waved for Jimmy.

Jimmy stepped inside, where Buddy sat in his wheelchair by a tub. Jimmy helped him disrobe, picked him up, and lowered his paralyzed body into the water. It was cold, so very cold—53.6 degrees Fahrenheit. The attendant crossed himself and offered in French an invocation to Our Lady of Lourdes and St. Bernadette.

Quickly, Jimmy then withdrew Buddy from the tub. Buddy was shivering.

Jimmy grabbed a towel and began drying him. But the attendant stepped between them and said, "No! No! No!" Jimmy understood that he was trying to say that he was supposed to allow the air to dry Buddy.

Neither of them knew how this whole thing worked, when or if Buddy was supposed to walk. So they laughed and went on their way, Jimmy pushing the frail body of his brother up a street as Buddy observed into the tape recorder, "Here come a parade of wheelchairs." To which Jimmy added sorrowfully, "A bunch of Buddys." They attended mass (Buddy said, "You would love it, Mom"), stopped by some souvenir shops, and headed back to the hotel. There, they had a ham-and-cheese sandwich for dinner, then stayed up well into the evening, laughing so hard that the occupant in the neighboring room pounded on the wall and shouted, "Keep it down in there!" The following day, they found their way back to the airport, where Jimmy hoisted Buddy out of his wheelchair on the tarmac and carried him up the steep stairwell to the plane. Jimmy could feel his grip loosen. Buddy looked down and said, "My pants are falling down!" But Jimmy eyed the cabin door up ahead and continued to climb, breathing hard as he replied, "Too bad!"

Gone just four days, they were ecstatic to be back, even if the trip seemed to have been for naught. Immediately, Jimmy stopped off for a can of Pringles and a gallon of milk. With the baseball season over, he worked during the week and cut loose on the weekend. Something was always going on. Two weeks or so later—on October 29—he joined some friends at a bar in Lambertville, New Jersey, where the drinking age then was only eighteen. In the back of his used Ford Pinto, the car he had gotten with his small bonus from the Dodgers, he had with him a case of beer, which he and a friend had worked down to a six-pack by the time they got to the bar at 10:00 P.M. or so. There, they drank rum-and-Cokes for another four hours and, shooed out the door at closing, piled in the car and headed off in search of a party.

Two girls they had met that evening were in a car behind them. They would see the whole thing: With his friend in the passenger seat, Jimmy was driving along, not erratically or fast, when he failed to negotiate a left curve in the road. The Pinto crashed into a tree. When the police arrived on the scene, they found the dazed passenger inside the wreck but not Jimmy. One of them asked, "Where is the driver?" The passenger, who had an injured back that would eventually heal, pointed to a concrete wall some seventy-five yards away. At the base of it, Jimmy lay unconscious, blood spilling from a head wound. The police ascertained that Jimmy had been hurled from his car door upon impact and hit the wall headfirst. They also discovered that he had a blood alcohol level of .24, or three times the legal limit.

Sleepily, Bert Miley answered the phone call that came in at 6:00 A.M. from Temple University Hospital. When the family convened there later that day, they were told by a worried doctor that Jimmy was in critical condition. He had fractures to his skull, nose, and shoulder, along with assorted facial lacerations. Surgeons performed a left frontal craniotomy. With his head wrapped in bandages, he was scarcely recognizable. His mother sat in the waiting room and quietly prayed, *Hail Mary, full of grace* . . . just as she had done nine years before. It seemed unbelievable to her that here she was again, in another hospital with another son near death. But when she went home that evening, the phone rang quite late. On the line was the doctor, who said in an animated voice, "I never call like this but I wanted you to know that Jimmy regained consciousness and was able to remember his phone number when I asked for it." Everyone would say for years to come that it was a miracle that he survived. Even Buddy, who would always add with the laugh, "Yeah, the one *I* was supposed to get."

. . . . .

Buddy and Karen in Warminster, 1984.
CREDIT: KAREN KOLLMEYER ARCHIVE

THIRTEEN

Yellow Roses

One by one, the Florida passengers stepped from the Jetway, as Buddy craned his head and searched for her in the crowd. George Bushman, his neighbor, had driven him in the van that day to Philadelphia International Airport and remembers how Buddy kept checking himself in the rearview mirror. "Georgie," he asked, "how is my hair? Does it look okay?" With a grin, Bushman said, "Bud, you look great. Relax, man." But Buddy could not relax. For years he had pictured this day and was overcome with giddiness now that it was upon him, even if it was not occurring as he had once promised Karen it would: with him showing up and sweeping her up into his arms. God, he had told her, he had been in such sad shape when he had last seen her, drugged up and scarcely able to even wear clothes. More than once he had asked himself in the intervening years, *How could I have let her go?*

Close to nine years had passed, yet Karen still appeared the same when he spotted her, at a certain angle reminiscent of the actress Lindsay Wagner in the popular TV show *The Bionic Woman.* Karen had that look: slender yet statuesque, with cascading blond hair and deep brown eyes. Bushman remembers, "Buddy did not date unattractive women." Bushman would take him for an outing at Willow Grove Mall, and when Buddy eyed a woman who appealed to him, he would say, "Georgie, wheel me over there." He would strike up a conversation just like that, perhaps even persuade the woman to have a seat on his lap. Women would come and go, some staying longer than others, yet Karen stirred feelings in Buddy that no one else did. With her baby daughter in tow, Karen smiled shyly, gave him a tentative hug and kiss. Few words passed between them as she pushed his wheelchair to the parking lot, where they settled into the van for the trip to Warminster.

Karen sat in the front seat with sunglasses on.

Buddy sat in the back with the baby, his wheelchair bolted to the floor.

Bushman drove.

Buddy asked Karen, "Is the sun too bright for you?"

"No, I'm fine," she said.

Buddy asked again, "Are you sure the sun is not too bright for you?"

"It's bright but I have sunglasses on."

Bushman chuckled.

Buddy asked yet again, "But are you sure?"

Exasperated, but certain that something playful was in the works, Karen said, "Buddy, I'm fine. What are you guys up to?"

By then both Buddy and Bushman were laughing. "Karen," Buddy said, "pull down your visor!"

So she did.

And a yellow rose fell into her lap.

"Jesus," Buddy said. "It's hard to surprise you."

Karen could not remember how long it had been since anyone had given her a yellow rose, perhaps not since Buddy himself had asked a nurse to bring her one at Sacred Heart Hospital. Since she had gone to Florida with her parents, her life had veered off into some wayward places. To begin with, college had to be delayed due to another kidney surgery in St. Petersburg, a place that she found to be devoid of young people (or, as she would call it, "the Home of the Newly Wed and Nearly Dead"). Tom Shields, her brother, remembers that the move from Pennsylvania left her "depressed beyond belief." To help her out of it, he acquainted her with the youth group of a charismatic Catholic church to which he belonged. Karen became popular there. Says Tom, "Karen was older than the other teenagers, beloved by everyone. Beloved." She became a mentor to troubled teens. But at eighteen she was still young and found herself in a secretive relationship with a man twice her age. In the year they were together, he became obsessed with her. When she broke it off, he called her to his home to remove a handgun—and with it, any temptation to use it on himself. He pleaded for her to marry him and invited her to leave with him the following morning for Las Vegas. She declined. The chaotic episode lingered with unanswered phone calls and unopened letters.

She found sanctuary in a friendship with a man she had come to know through church. John was eleven years older, just discharged from the service, and a student at the University of South Florida. Karen had a small apartment in St. Petersburg and supported herself as a church secretary. John moved in. When Karen quit her job and John dropped out of school, they headed to Michigan, where John had brothers and was certain they could both find work. Initially, Karen embraced the move, if just to flee the persistent attentions of her spurned suitor. There was a stop in Grand Rapids—which Karen hated—and then it was on to Traverse City, a picturesque settlement with panoramic views of the bay that Karen discovered one day on a drive by herself. Against the wishes of her parents, who foresaw problems in the relationship and offered Karen the $10,000 cost of the wedding in cash to call it off, John and Karen were married in February 1977 in a ceremony back in Florida. For a period they remained in Michigan, where John worked for a cable company and Karen sold Levi's in a shop, only to settle back in Largo, Florida, where in 1981 they had a daughter, Jessica. Karen attended nursing school and moved back in with her parents when she and John separated. They later divorced.

Karen remembers that she was standoffish when she first saw Buddy at the airport. But she would always be that way whenever she saw him again, uncertain of both the condition he would be in and how she should act until Buddy would grin and say, "Come on, Karen. It's *me*." While they had not seen each other since 1974, they had spoken occasionally on the telephone—once or twice or so a year in the beginning, less frequently as the years passed. When they did, Karen remembers they spoke as if they were just "old high school buddies," albeit with an undercurrent of having once shared something special. Generally, Buddy evinced no deep interest in her personal relationships—only her—yet when he contacted her in the spring of 1982, he had been told by someone that she and her husband had separated. Word circulated that it had been an acrimonious parting. Always, Buddy was protective of Karen and leaped to her defense, as any man would for the woman that he loved. Friend Pat Delaney says, "When he heard she had been mistreated, Buddy was fucking livid."

No one had the ability to alleviate his pain the way Karen did. Hearing her voice again was better than the occasional shot of Southern Comfort he took, or the pills that left him so spaced-out (which is why he always resisted taking them). Whenever she spoke with him, her voice soothed him, just as surely as hearing his father yak in the other room would leave him shaking with spasms. While no

one can ever know why Buddy taped the conversations with Karen—
apparently with the help of Jimmy, who says, "I was always doing the
sneaky stuff"—those who knew him assumed that he did so to cap-
ture her voice so that he could play it back and transport himself to a
place of calm. Medically, Guy Fried, the CMO at Magee Rehab, says
there is evidence that hearing the voice of a loved one is an analgesic.
"Love distracts," says Fried. "People who are in love feel less pain.
This is true of anyone. If I am lying there and I feel hopeless and there
is a sensory deprivation where no one is talking to me, I can only feel
the pain. It becomes a water torture, the heartbeat in 'The Tell-Tale
Heart' by Edgar Allan Poe—you are hearing it over and over and over
again. You are locked within that pain, and that is all you are feeling.
But a loving voice becomes very soothing."

Choosing to see Buddy again always posed a conundrum for
Karen. On one hand, her feelings for him had remained strong—
that had not changed in the years they had been apart, and as always,
they were imbued with her hopes for him. The bond that developed
between them so long ago enabled her, once the initial uneasiness
passed, to pick up where they had left off and fall into easy conversation. Karen remembers, "From the first moment we settled in to
having our time alone, it was as if we were two kids again with everything in life to look forward to." But Karen understood the power
that he had conferred upon her, and how it had the potential to leave
him either giddy with joy or so very, very sad. In the phone call that
he had taped, early on the air of casualness he exuded evaporated
into searching desperation, and he would go places that would leave
Karen unsure what to do or say. But the tension that had attended
that initial conversation seemed to settle in the next, as Buddy convinced her that he was fine—even better than fine. "He just sounded
good," Karen says. "He had strength in his voice. I could always tell
how he was doing by his voice. You could hear the pain in it. Or the

lack of it. We talked about the year we spent together in high school, and how it helped get both of us through that part of life. I wanted to see him again. I wanted to see him doing well and feeling strong." Karen remembers that she had wondered for years how he was doing and was encouraged to hear that he had a business under way and that through rehab he had achieved some independence. As their conversations unfolded, Karen says, "We became close again, and he asked me to come to see him once he and Jimmy returned from Lourdes." Buddy sent her a necklace from Lourdes, with a cross blessed in the healing waters.

Given the troubles that had engulfed her, it would seem fair to say that to some extent Karen found safe harbor once again with Buddy. Being with him, it was always easy to slip back into the deep feelings he had for her. "The first thing that always pops into my head when I think of him is how we always just laughed," Karen says. But it was not simply that. Buddy looked upon her with an unconditional affection, of which Karen adds, "I never had to worry about a thing I did or said, whether it was something he agreed with or not. Buddy was so giving of himself. I was far less so. I had friends, people always liked me, but I was always protective and only showed the world bits and pieces. But Buddy would insist on knowing more. He would say, 'Karen, you are holding back.' And that was something I always loved about him. Because he wanted to know me, what I was *really* thinking. And I would always dig deeper, because of how he was always so open." No one else she would ever know had the ability to peer into her heart with such unobstructed clarity.

Going back to the house on Acorn Drive was in a certain way for Karen like stepping back to 1973. Bert and Rosemarie had aged some. Both of them greeted her cordially. Other than Buddy, only Jimmy still lived in the house—the others had gone off to jobs or marriages. But Jimmy was scarcely a presence in the wake of his accident, given that he lived in the basement as he convalesced from an additional surgery to insert a plate in his head; he had a black patch over one eye and blurred vision in the other. Buddy had his "bachelor's pad," where his mother set up a crib for Jessica and a cot for Karen. Karen remembers that Rosemarie was especially welcoming to her, that she always had something in the refrigerator for her and she appreciated how she lent an extra hand with Buddy. Offhandedly, Rosemarie told her with a giggle how wonderful it was to sit down and have an uninterrupted glass of iced tea. Karen clearly saw that Rosemarie was bearing the weight of unrelenting responsibility—and doing it extraordinarily well. Even when Buddy became edgy with her when she did not attend to him in a timely manner, she approached him with what appeared to be an inexhaustible sense of humor.

Karen came up twice for ten-day stays in 1983—during that spring break from St. Petersburg Junior College, and again in the fall. During the latter visit, they attended an Eagles game, where Buddy had been invited to take part in a charitable initiative organized by the club, Eagles Fly for Leukemia. Karen remembers they sat in a private box, that Buddy did some television interviews; he asked her to join him but she was camera shy and stood in the back. But Buddy embraced the uninterrupted interludes between the two of them, how each morning they would discuss what was in the papers; or how they would sit at the table and eat the sandwiches she had prepared for them; or how they would sit in front of the TV and eat popcorn. In the evening they would take strolls together in the neighborhood or head off to the park. Proudly, Buddy would introduce her to passersby: "This is Karen, my high school girlfriend. I should have married her!" None of it seemed to Karen to be beyond just "normal stuff," what friends did with and for one another, yet for Buddy these acts were building blocks of something larger—the apotheosis of love. Nothing pleased him more than to overhear Karen and his mother laughing over a cup

of coffee in the kitchen, and before long Buddy had come to think of
Jessica as his own daughter.

Just by being together again, they would step back into the same
lovely bubble they had occupied years before, in some place where innocence and possibility had remained unaltered. When they were
alone in his room with the sliding door closed, it was as if they were
back at Sacred Heart Hospital, where they had created a world that
existed beyond the pain and the indignity that had swept into his life.
Ten years later, that world emerged once again in the starless universe
that had enveloped him, and Buddy layered upon it a parallel history
in which he imagined what it would be like if he and Karen had been
wed. Karen remembers, "Buddy would always go into extensive de-
tail, how he would always treat me like a queen." No day with him
would be without yellow roses.

Lying with her in his bed, he told her, We would have dinner
parties.

And here are the people we would invite.

And this is what you would wear.

And this is how you would wear your hair.

It would be like the virtual vacations they used to take to some
sunny beach. Buddy would have their whole day planned: when the
sun would come up, how long they would stay in bed, where they
would go, how he would take care of the children. On and on he would
go, and as the words spilled from him, it became clear that he had
become ambulatory again, that he had stepped through some passage
in his imagination that allowed him to slip the bonds of his paralysis.
Karen remembers, "As he spoke, he would cease to be an injured
man. I used to worry that he kept me in the 1970s, and that he was
attaching me to something that was not real."

Grinning, Buddy told her, "This is what it would be like. This is
how I would treat you."

"Buddy," she said, "don't fool yourself, it is never that way when you live with someone day after day. You have bad days. People get grouchy with each other. They get tired of each other."

"No. That would never happen. That is not even possible. No one would ever treat you the way I would."

Inevitably, the subject of where this was heading came up. But it only did so briefly and in a casual way at first. In a conversation the evening before Karen would fly back to Florida, Buddy slipped again into reverie, speaking of how different life would be for them "if only." She could see that he was preparing himself for her to leave and wondering if she would again disappear from his life. Given that Karen was then obtaining a divorce, it seemed to Buddy that if they ever had a chance to get together, it would be now. The way he envisioned it, Karen would finish up school, move up to Warminster with Jessica, and get a job at one of the countless hospitals in the Philadelphia area. Until they found their own place, she and Jessica could move into the house on Acorn Drive. While Buddy did not immediately reveal his plans before Karen left, the conversation they had was such that Karen became concerned. Gently she told him, "Buddy, I cannot see this happening. I don't know how it could." They spoke of how their lives had changed in ten years. But she did not come out and just say *never,* and that was one of the problems Karen always had when it came to Buddy. "It was nearly impossible to deny him these places where he found comfort," she says. Invariably, she would lose her objectivity whenever they were together. Karen remembers, "We loved our time together, we had such fun in our own little world, that I would fall in love with him again. He was easy to love and it was easy to be in the places he created for me. Visits were always hard in the end because leaving him was always heartbreaking. We never knew when or if we would see each other again."

Clarity only came when some space was between them. Karen

had a baby and the responsibility of caring for her. How could she do that, work, and still care for Buddy? With her divorce not yet final, Karen could not separate Jessica from her father in Florida, nor did she want to. Moreover, Karen had seen during her visits just how physically exhausting it had been for Rosemarie to take care of Buddy—indeed, how it took the entire Miley family to meet his needs. But now that she had a child, Karen understood that the deep feelings she had for Buddy were not the same as one would have for a son or a daughter. Moreover—and this would ultimately play into her thinking—Buddy "oversold" how well his business was going and the independence that it brought him. He had balked at undergoing rehabilitation that would have enabled him to acquire some autonomy to feed himself and perform other similar activities of daily living. For as long as he lived, Buddy would be in need of total care. Karen says, "I just knew that it was more than I could do, especially with a daughter to care for. No degree of love would ever change that.

"Was it something I considered? Yes. It was. Because I knew how deeply he wanted this and how much he wanted to love and be loved. I loved him. I loved to see him happy, and I knew he was able to override his pain when we were together. I cared what happened to him and understood the torment of what he had lost. However, I hoped and I believed that if he could have had a truly loving friendship with me, I could have been good for him. Because I could calm him down. The problem was that he could see me as nothing short of his wife. And that is what he believed our lives should have been. But that was not something I could give him."

Buddy believed he could talk her into it—he always believed that—and that led to a series of excruciating phone calls. The conversations would begin casually enough, with how her day had gone and such, but soon he would ask, "When are you coming up?" Karen told him she planned to stay in Florida and told him why, but her words seemed to pass over him. They would be on the phone for what sometimes seemed like hours, at the end of which Karen believed he understood and that they had come to some accord. But two days later it would be as if the conversation had not even occurred. Buddy would say, with the edge of desperation in his voice that always alarmed her, "I just know you would stay if you came up." Karen remembers, "To say no to him over and over and over again just destroyed me, because saying no was something I had never wanted to do to this man I cared for." For Karen, it had always been a calculation of how painful her presence had become to him, if it had commenced to outweigh the pleasure he had derived from it. Karen says, "I had always wanted to help take the pain away from him, and not be a source of it for him."

Still living with her parents, Karen found a one-room apartment in Indian Rocks Beach, a block from the Gulf of Mexico. When she moved out, her mother asked her what she should do if Buddy called: "Should I give him your number?" Karen told her no. "Good," Janet Shields said, "I wouldn't have given him the number anyway." Karen said, "Well, now you have my permission." Buddy called once and was told by Janet that Karen had her own place and had asked her not to give out her number. As the days passed and Warminster became a memory again, Karen settled into her $8-per-hour job at Largo Medical Center and would each evening take Jessica for a walk along the beach. It was a nice time in their lives—just the two of them—yet Karen would think of Buddy and the way she had just dropped out of his life, and it would leave her feeling as if she had wronged him, as if she had taken the easy way out. But she could not think of what else she could have done, and that would prey upon her for years.

"19 Years of Hell," Philadelphia Daily News, 1993.

FOURTEEN

. . . . .

Longing

It seemed to happen every year: Another young man would end up just like Buddy, the victim of a game that his mother had come to abhor. Whenever Rosemarie would open the newspaper and see an account of an incident that had occurred to a high school, college, or pro player, the good humor she always exuded would fall away, and with a sigh she would think, *God in heaven, here we go again!* Near the end of November 1992, it happened yet again: New York Jets defensive end Dennis Byrd fractured his C5 vertebra in a game against the Kansas City Chiefs and was paralyzed from the chest down. On newsstands the following week, *Sports Illustrated* carried a story on the escalation of injuries in the NFL that season with a cover line that announced, "The Carnage Continues." Rosemarie had never written a letter to the editor of any publication, nor had she written more than an occasional letter to anyone since she used to cheer up the troops back in the 1940s.

But she not could sit idly any longer. Someone had to do something. She sat down at the table with a piece of paper, jotted down a few paragraphs, and gave it to her son Bob, who had a colleague at school look it over for spelling and grammar. She then found the address for *Sports Illustrated,* placed the letter in a stamped envelope and dropped it in the mailbox. Given that the weekly receives hundreds upon hundreds of such correspondences, she did not expect to see it again. But there it was, on page 14 of the January 18, 1993, issue.

> *My son broke his neck 19 years ago playing high school*
> *football. Since then our home has been hell on earth. The*
> *injury has altered forever the life of our family and the lives of*
> *our son's friends. I am sure the majority of* SI *readers "love"*
> *football. I ask them to spend one day with my son. They will see*
> *the terrible pain he endures. They will feel his frustration at*
> *being totally dependent on others.*
>
> *The NFL seems to glamorize bone-jarring hits and on-*
> *field violence. Instead, shouldn't the league donate some of its*
> *profits to aid research into spinal-cord injuries? And shouldn't it*
> *take strong measures to reduce the occurrence of these on-field*
> *injuries?*
>
> ROSEMARIE MILEY
Warminster, Pa.

Through this letter, I became acquainted with Buddy Miley. An editor at the paper where I worked, the *Philadelphia Daily News,* handed me a copy of it and seemed to think there could be an interesting piece there—one that could bring a local angle to what had become a national story in the wake of the Byrd injury. While I had not heard of Buddy—I had only arrived in Philadelphia a few years earlier—I could see from the clip file that his story had been told before, that he had become an obligatory stop whenever the debate over football violence had heated up. Old ground, it seemed at a glance, yet when I looked at the *SI* letter again, I could not help but be drawn in by the colossal struggle that had engulfed Rosemarie and her dare that summoned the world to Warminster to look at what football had done to her boy.

So that Sunday I drove out to see him. In my memory, it was a cold January day, windy, the winter sun glaring off the windshield of my car. From my home in South Jersey, it was an hour or so easily: across the Delaware River, off one expressway and onto another, then exiting onto a boulevard that passed by a series of shopping centers, the Willow Grove Naval Air Station, and then back into a subdivision of Eisenhower-era ranchers, where the Miley house sat at the corner of Acorn and Kingsley. There, Rosemarie greeted me at the door and walked me in to see Buddy, propped up in his bed by a window that looked out on a street that once teemed with children but was now vacant. In blue jeans and a brown sweater with white stripes on the sleeves, which he sported over a white turtleneck that climbed up beneath his bearded chin, he was perfectly groomed, every hair in place, as if he had just walked out of a barbershop.

It would be his birthday in a few days.

On January 28, he would be thirty-seven.

We were the same age.

Nineteen-plus years had passed since that September day in 1973—better than seven thousand days. On the day Buddy was injured, I had been a junior at a high school in Baltimore. I had played some sports, but not well, and I had steered clear of football, for no other reason than it seemed too damned dangerous; I had a few sprains here and there, but never a broken bone. Time had stopped for Buddy, but it proceeded for me undeterred, with enough good moments to offset the inevitable disappointments that came along. In the years that seemed as if they had passed in a blur, I had dropped out of college, broken up with girlfriends, gotten a newspaper job, become engaged, gotten another newspaper job, married, moved to Philadelphia, and had the first of two daughters. At various junctures, I had struggled with father issues, career issues, and addiction issues, which would send me spiraling into a deep depression and leave me explaining to a psychiatrist, "I feel as if I have turned to stone." What Buddy would have given for any of it, even the lowest of what seemed to me to be days steeped in unrelenting gloom. How he would gladly have exchanged the soaring expectations he once had for the opportunity to be just average; to have legs to carry him whenever he pleased, and arms to hold the people he loved.

An NFL game was on the TV in his room when I got there. Far from looking upon the sport with the disdain that his mother did, Buddy still enjoyed watching football and even placed small wagers with the local bookie on the college and pro card each Saturday and Sunday. Jimmy used to drive him out to high school games, and he was always talking on the phone with the area coaches; they often discussed strategies, personnel, and such. In an interview once, Buddy was even quoted as saying, "If I could put on the pads, I would." Up on the shelves that Dave Heilbrun had wrangled from the local furniture store years before were pieces of sports memorabilia he had grown fond of: signed baseballs; jerseys, caps, and bats; photographs of his encounters with a variety of sports stars. On the shelf there was also a Holy Bible.

With a pillow behind his head, Buddy appeared eager for the company, even if it would be for an interview that he had done before and would do again. Friends still stopped by occasionally, he told me, but with less and less frequency than they had years before, when the house had been filled with visitors. Boys he had grown up with now had wives and children—some were even on their second marriages. "People just drift away," he said. "That is the disappointing part of life, but it is a part I have come to accept." But people still dropped in to see him: Guy Driesbach would come by every other Sunday if he could; and Brian Sheehan would swing by at the end of his jog though the neighborhood; and there was always Vinnie Medveckus—"Vinnie the Mailman"—who would stop by each day on his rounds, talk, use the bathroom, talk some more, and be on his way. In the warm weather they would sit outside on the porch; Buddy loved being outdoors.

Casually, he asked me if I would like to see the Play. What I would come to learn is that he was apt to ask this of new visitors, as if by replaying it again and again he could spot something he had not seen before—the crack in the earth that had swallowed him up. When I told him I would, he called to Rosemarie, "Mom, can you put the tape of the game in?" She did not have to ask which one. She slid a cassette into the VCR, and suddenly the NFL game disappeared from the screen, replaced by the grainy, black-and-white footage of that 1973 game between William Tennent and Plymouth Whitemarsh. There was no sound, only a sequence of plays captured from a camera somewhere high above the field. From the vantage point of his bed, Buddy looked upon himself then as if he were trying to remember how it had been, not just to play but to have full authority over his body. There he is, standing over center, with his black shoes wrapped in adhesive tape. There he is, hitting Craig White in the end zone for what would be his final touchdown pass. And there he is, tucking the ball under his arm, turning upfield, and—in an eye blink—vanishing from view under a pile of tacklers, as if he had been a capsized surfer churned under by a collapsing wave. Gazing upon it now with a faraway look, he told me that he had begun hearing an odd "sizzling noise," how it began in the soles of his feet and shot upward through his legs, torso, and arms before stopping just below his chin.

"I knew I was going to die," he told me. "I said to myself, 'Thank you, Lord, for giving me seventeen years of life. I am ready to go now.' I could feel my soul leaving my body and I started up into this tunnel of white light. Things were so peaceful." He lowered his eyes. "Then . . . well . . . the brakes got slammed on somehow. I remember looking up and seeing the coaches and players huddled over me."

What had it been: God calling him home or—as a skeptic would have it—the biology of his oxygen-deprived brain shutting down? Given his upbringing, Buddy favored the former explanation and ended each day with a prayer that God would allow him to continue his journey into that "white light" and that place of peace. But eight hours later he would open his eyes and still be there—in that bed and in that room—the seconds building into days and then weeks and years. No one captured the physical captivity that Buddy endured better than his brother Bob, who later told me, "Try it yourself: Sit in one place for an hour and not move, not if you have an itch or even if you have to go to the bathroom. Now imagine doing that for years." While Buddy remained unwavering in his belief in God, a part of him wondered what possible purpose there could be for his suffering. In the eleven years that had passed since he had come back from Lourdes, it seemed as if every visitor who stopped by had assured him there had to be some divine plan that he was part of, especially the Catholic clergy that looked in on him. Solace had even come from Anthony Cardinal Bevilacqua, who spent close to an hour in private with Buddy, even shooing away aides who reminded him he had a schedule to keep. The cardinal told a congregation he addressed that evening, "I was in the presence of a saint today."

Buddy was unraveling by degrees. Everyone could see it, but few knew what to say; Bill Juzwiak, his old football coach, began to feel the conviction ebb from his own voice as he assured Buddy again and again, "Something good will happen." What it came down to was the damn pain that coursed through his body . . . if only he could have been spared that. He would never know when it would strike, only that it would—and in uncontrollable spasms. Early on, according to his friend Mary Jane Williams, he would just "grit his teeth" and say he was fine. He would do whatever he could to spare visitors even a glimpse of himself in that state. But it had become hard for him to keep it in, and he would have to ask them to leave. Mary Jane remembers how she would be on the telephone with him when an attack started and he would begin to gasp for air. But he had other physical ailments, the attrition that comes from years of immobility: the recurrence of bedsores (Rosemarie was assiduous in doing whatever she could to prevent them) and a problem with kidney stones, which Driesbach says prevented Buddy from serving as the best man at his wedding. Driesbach adds, "You could see that he was wearing down."

I could see on the day I interviewed him that he was also worried. Years and years of caring for him had been hard on Rosemarie, and he could see how it weighed on her whenever she walked into the room, always with a sparkle of cheer in her eye yet with an increasing exhaustion that had become palpable. With charming vanity, Rosemarie had told me when I had asked her age, "Oh, no, please! The old gray mare is not what she used to be." With no appreciable help from her husband, who generally occupied his own space and looked on from a far remove, not unlike how he'd looked down from the window of his plane upon that burning city in Japan years before, Rosemarie had soldiered on with the help of her other now-grown children. She had vowed that she would not let Buddy out of her care the way she had Nana, who was well into her nineties when Rosemarie had placed her in a nursing home. But Rosemarie was having health problems herself: Osteoporosis had so weakened her that she had broken eight bones within the last year. Buddy told me, "The woman is so strong. I see her in pain and it just kills me." The dwindling funds in a foundation that had been set up for Buddy were used to bring in a nurse at $100 per week, but Rosemarie could foresee a day when they could no longer afford even that. Of even greater concern, she asked, "What will happen when we die? Who is going to take care of him? What happens to Buddy then?"

Money had been an endless concern in the years since Buddy had been injured. Even with the good health plan Bert had at Exide—which early on covered the hospital stay and other expenses—and the disability checks that came in from Medicaid, somehow another bill always seemed to show up out of nowhere. To help out, close friends such as Sheehan organized occasional "beef-and-beers," golf outings, and other charitable events on behalf of Buddy, whose proceeds went to the Buddy Miley Foundation. The account never held a large sum, but enough to pay for his van, wheelchair, and travel expenses in and out of state for consultations with doctors. But as challenging as it would become to stretch a dollar, not once did Rosemarie or Bert or even Buddy second-guess their decision not to have filed a lawsuit in the wake of the injury, even when it became clear that there had been errors in the care Buddy had received. In fact, Rosemarie says that years later she ran into a former school-board member who expressed surprise that no lawsuit had been launched. The woman told her that they had been expecting it. But Rosemarie says, "No one was to blame for what happened, and suing someone was not who we are."

Buddy blamed no one either, but would say occasionally to Karen and others, "Can you believe how they handled me on the field?" And he would just chuckle.

I would come to think just how unaccountably cruel the timing of his injury had been. In one moment, he had been full of energy and ego, the blood coursing through his tall, athletic body, not a concern in the universe but what was happening that very second. In another moment, he was on the ground, his central nervous system unplugged, left with a body that no longer worked but with a mind that carried a cupboard full of memories of how it used to feel to hold the world in his hands. Buddy had seventeen years to look back on and remember: of gripping a football in his hand, his long fingers crawling up over the laces; of scooping a spoonful of peanut butter out of a jar and spreading it across a piece of bread; of stealing away to his basement hideaway with a young woman and experiencing the exquisite pleasures of touch. None of this would ever again be possible, and yet, as our day came to a close, I sensed that he could not bring himself to let go of the young man he once was, that an essential piece of him remained anchored in 1973. When we said good-bye, I remember as I drove home thinking of what he had told me: Being unable to walk was not the hardest part. The hardest part was the longing.

The story appeared in the paper on his birthday under the title "19 Years of Hell." With it was a photograph of Buddy seated in his wheelchair by his window, accompanied by a quote from him: "There are days I wake up in dread, thinking, 'Not another day of this.'" Some years later this story would help Buddy solve that problem, but its immediate impact temporarily buoyed him. Contributions poured into the fund again—$32,000 in total, including $11,000 from an anonymous donor. Even better, friends he had not seen in years began calling or showing up again, including Pat Delaney. Well off by now, Delaney organized a fund-raiser to enable Buddy to see the specialists at the Miami Project to Cure Paralysis. One of the people Delaney invited was Carmen Frangiosa, who had, Delaney remembered, seemed standoffish. Delaney had known him since they were boys and says, "Carmen seemed really touchy." *Uneasy* would be a better word, Frangiosa says, if only because he could not escape the feeling that he had been "the guy"—the one who'd placed Buddy in his wheelchair. Ordinarily, Frangiosa would chat with Buddy briefly at these functions and leave. But on that evening Buddy could sense the pain Frangiosa was in.

"How are you?" Buddy asked.

Frangiosa eyed him sadly. "It just pisses me off, Buddy. It really does. We could've been like so many guys we played against. We should've been playing golf together."

Buddy smiled. "You should know, I got this injury years ago. Back when I was playing for the Little Quakers. I hurt my neck."

"What?"

"Yeah, something cracked and never healed properly, I guess. No one ever knew because I never told anyone."

Frangiosa remembers that conversation. "Immediately, it was as if a weight had been lifted off my shoulders—as if I had been absolved in some way. But I looked at him and he said, 'Everything hurts, Carmen. They're never going to come up with a cure for this.'"

But Buddy flew to Miami for an appointment at the Miami Project, the leading research center in the world for the treatment of paralysis. Joining Buddy on the trip were his sister Patti, her husband, Rudy, and their three-year-old son, Shane. Rudy remembers, "He was just looking for something that would ease his pain." But that was not to be had. In a critical way, he had come along too late—indeed during "the dark time"—before the advances in treatment that would enable Dennis Byrd to recover and coauthor his autobiography, *Rise & Walk: The Trial and Triumph of Dennis Byrd*. But Buddy would neither rise nor walk, and the doctors in Miami told him what his other doctors had advised: *You just have to bite the bullet*. On their way out of the hospital that day, a friendly nurse recommended a beach that they should see, so they piled into their rental and drove over to it. There, Rudy unfolded the wheelchair, strapped Buddy in it, and began pushing through the sand toward the edge of the Atlantic Ocean, which seemed to go on forever under the Florida sun. Suddenly, Buddy looked up at Rudy and said, "Are you seeing what I'm seeing?" Girls were everywhere, and none of them had tops on. Over the objections of Patti, Buddy urged Rudy, "Keep pushing!"

I could just picture him laughing his ass off that day on South Beach.

We only spoke once again—just a casual chat—but Buddy did show up in the news two years later. That December 1995 story involved Buddy and Yvonne Ameche, the friendship that had blossomed between them, and an act of generosity that was undermined by what Yvonne calls "a crime against humanity." Retelling it, it seems hard to know where the beginning is, if it began with the event that transpired, or if it began years and years before under whatever black cloud had settled on that unassuming house on Acorn Drive. Nothing had ever gone right for Buddy, and this surely seemed to prove it.

No one had given more generously of his heart than Alan Ameche, so there is some cruel irony in that he could not get another one when he needed it. He had battled cardiovascular disease for years, but it became clear by age fifty-five that he would have to have a transplant if he hoped to see fifty-six. Upon flying to Houston, he reminded Yvonne, the girl he'd once carried on his handlebars back in Kenosha, "Just think, if something happens to me, I will be with our son Paul. And I will get to meet Beethoven." But he had one of the top cardiac surgeons in the world—Dr. Michael E. DeBakey—and every expectation was that a heart would become available, given that it was the weekend and fatal car wrecks frequently occur then. But none did and Ameche died that Monday.

Early loss had been a recurring event for Yvonne: There were her parents, who passed away at ages forty-nine and fifty-one; her sister had succumbed at forty-four; Paul was just twenty-two when he died in a automobile accident . . . "Oh, that was the hardest of any of them"; and now her husband, thirty-seven years together . . . the love of her life. Standing up on the altar prior to the funeral, Yvonne spotted Buddy in the crowd at the church; he had come with his parents. Yvonne walked down to say hello. Buddy eyed her worriedly and said, "I hope you'll be okay." Yvonne did not think more of it than just an earnest condolence, yet before long Buddy called her, not once but periodically, to ask, "Are you okay?" So one day she set aside the apprehensions she once had and drove out to see him—or as she remembers, "To prove to him that I was okay." On a subsequent visit during the 1993 Christmas season, she gave him a white football autographed by fourteen Heisman Trophy recipients. Someone placed it up on the shelf with some of the other stuff he had, but he would come to look upon it as an item unlike any other, not because of its value as a piece of memorabilia but as a symbol of a relationship that had become so meaningful to him.

They had wonderful fun adding signatures to the ball. Whenever Yvonne would go on a trip where she expected to run into a Heisman Trophy winner, she would stop by the house, pick up the ball, and take it with her. Eight more autographs were added by the end of the year, bringing the total up to more than twenty. On it were the elite players in the history of college football: Jay Berwanger and Larry Kelley, the first and second winners in 1935 and 1936, respectively; Glenn Davis, Johnny Lujack, Leon Hart, Johnny Lattner, Billy Cannon, Joe Bellino, Roger Staubach, John Huarte, Steve Spurrier, Steve Owens, Archie Griffin, Tony Dorsett, Herschel Walker, Mike Rozier, and others. Buddy even arranged with a childhood friend who worked for NBC Sports to obtain the autograph of O. J. Simpson just two weeks before he was arrested in connection with the slaying of his former wife and a male friend. The ball had become irreplaceable.

Yvonne took it that December to the annual Heisman Trophy

affair at the Downtown Athletic Club in New York. Given that Ameche had been the 1954 winner, she always attended the event. It was good to catch up with old friends, especially when everyone gathered for Family Night on Sunday. Yvonne had added four more autographs to the ball that weekend and brought it with her that evening just in case she came across someone else whose signature she had still not gotten. Some three hundred or so people were there, a big crowd, and Yvonne stepped away from her seat at the banquet table to see a friend she noticed. She placed the ball under the table, hidden behind a floor-length tablecloth. When she returned, it was gone. She searched everywhere, but it had vanished. Somebody had stolen Buddy's ball.

Someone
to
Turn To

. . . . .

Buddy.

. . . . .

FIFTEEN

Dr. Death

Millions of words would be spent on the subject of Dr. Jack Kevorkian—on his behalf and at his expense—yet society would never come close to a consensus. Always, he would be looked upon either as a fiery crusader on the side of self-determination or a genocidal egomaniac who seemed to have stepped down from one of the ghoulish canvases he was fond of painting. However he would be perceived in years to come, Kevorkian appeared to journalist Neal Rubin in March 1990 to be just "a heck of a good column." Rubin, who then wrote the Department of State column for the *Detroit Free Press* Sunday magazine, saw in a summary of reader calls to the *Free Press* ombudsman that Kevorkian had called to object that the paper would not publish a classified advertisement that he had wanted to place. From what Rubin could infer, the proposed ad had been a solicitation by Kevorkian for the incurably ill to contact him for his help in committing a physician-assisted suicide.

Rubin began calling around to see if anyone had a telephone

number for Kevorkian. It then occurred to Rubin to check directory assistance. Sure enough, as he later said, "The guy was in the book."

No one in the popular press had written about Kevorkian, who then was an anonymous pathologist who lived in a one-bedroom apartment above a clothing shop and favored a wardrobe that appeared to have been rescued from the Salvation Army. Rubin, a cheerful fellow with a keen eye for unusual characters and places, had hoped to do the interview with Kevorkian at his apartment in order to absorb some color. But Kevorkian instead had him come to the basement of the Royal Oak Public Library, where he busied himself each day researching articles on euthanasia for obscure journals. In a version of what would be looked upon as his customary attire—on that day a green, button-down sweater and double-knit slacks—he reminded Rubin of "an Armenian leprechaun." Gaunt, with a long, crooked nose and swept-back, white hair, Kevorkian placed his invention on the table between them. He called it a Thanatron—an allusion to Thanatos, the personification of death in Greek mythology.

Apparently, he had been tinkering with the apparatus for some time, going through various versions of it. The one he showed Rubin had been cobbled together with a scrap of aluminum and the motor from a toy car.

Three glass bottles were suspended from a simple frame, twenty inches high and fourteen inches across.

Drip: In one would be a saline solution. That would keep the intravenous line open.

Drip: In the second would be thiopental. That would induce a coma.

Drip: In the third would be potassium chloride. That would stop the heart.

Kevorkian would attach the IV to the patient. The patient would then press the button, which would begin the flow of chemicals and precipitate death.

Curious, Rubin asked where he kept such a contraption.

Kevorkian told him, "In the bedroom closet on the floor."

"What else do you have in there?"

Kevorkian shrugged. "Oh, some shoes."

With Kevorkian for an hour that day, Rubin got an early earful of what would become the underpinnings of his rhetoric: Medicine, religion, and politics are full of "dark-age hypocrites"; euthanasia is a "positive thing . . . what good is anguish"; and the opponents that he expected would one day prosecute him are "philosophical cowards." Few commented on the emergence of this odd character when the column appeared on Sunday, March 18, 1990—Rubin remembered that there was "no strong response" to his piece—but that changed in June when Janet Adkins, a fifty-four-year-old Alzheimer's patient from Oregon, flew to Michigan with her husband and became the first volunteer to be hooked up by Kevorkian to his "suicide machine." In Portland preparing a piece on the city to appear during the NBA Finals between the Trail Blazers and the Detroit Pistons, Rubin was in the *Oregonian* newsroom when the story broke. "I remember I was standing over the shoulder of the assistant city editor as he scanned through my story on LexisNexis," says Rubin, currently a columnist for *The Detroit News*. "Everyone wanted to know, 'Who is this guy Jack Kevorkian?'"

That question was soon answered. As the 1990s unfolded, everyone would hear of Kevorkian, the son of Armenian immigrants who had escaped the massacres of the Ottoman Empire in the early twentieth century. In Michigan, deceased bodies began popping up everywhere, generally at motels and occasionally at the receiving-room door at hospitals. For both, he became an aggravation. A Kevorkian job was always, according to Rubin, "a huge pain in the butt," given that it summoned swarms of police cars and news trucks. In the more than 130 suicides that Kevorkian ultimately claimed to have assisted, he altered between lethal injection and the other device he favored, the Mercitron (or mercy machine), whereby the patient would inhale carbon monoxide through a gas mask. While Kevorkian claimed to abide by a code of strict guidelines of assisting only those who were verifiably terminal or in agonizing pain and only when assessed psychiatrically, the *Free Press* conducted an investigation in March 1997 that looked into the circumstances surrounding the deaths of the forty-seven patients Kevorkian had assisted at that point: More than half were not terminal, and Kevorkian had not contacted a psychiatrist in nineteen of the cases (in five of which there had been a history of depression). But with the State of Michigan bearing down on him—he would be indicted but not convicted on three occasions in the 1990s—Geoffrey N. Fieger, his attorney, said it was "not practical" for Kevorkian to follow the guidelines he said he endorsed. Fieger said Kevorkian was "at war."

Dr. Death: It is impossible to know how Buddy first came across him, whether it had been one of the countless television interviews Kevorkian was then doing or perhaps just a joke by Jay Leno ("The Michigan roads were so slippery that Kevorkian was leaving two dead bodies for extra traction!"). No one who had been close to Buddy remembered when it happened, just that one day he began dropping Kevorkian into the conversation, as if to ask, *What do you think?* But hearing this from him surprised no one. For years, he had pondered the possibility of committing suicide. It had been folded within whatever unattainable dreams had eluded him through the years: of walking again; of sweeping Karen off her feet; or of just living some semblance of a normal existence free of pain. Depression weighed on him in varying degrees, yet he did not seek psychological counseling, which he presumed would be as ineffective as the clonazepam that his doctors doled out to him to keep him calm. While the psychiatrist Donald L. Nathanson, M.D., did not treat Buddy—no one did—he observed, "For people who live in constant pain—a degree of pain where no painkiller gives them any feeling of relief—they commit suicide not to kill themselves but to stop the pain. What they are saying is, 'If I cannot end the pain, I can end me.'"

Going back to the very beginning, it was incomprehensible to Buddy that he could go on. At Sacred Heart Hospital, he asked his teammate, running back Bob McCarney, to help him out of his predicament. McCarney remembers that Buddy was then in traction, that two bolts had been drilled into his head and were attached to weights that held his spinal column in place. Buddy asked him, "Bobby, reach back there and pull the pin." Doing so would have unhooked him from the weights, which would have snapped his neck and killed him. McCarney told him, "Bud, there is no way I can do that." Once he got home from the hospital, Buddy seemed to have a better grip on himself, yet McCarney remembers standing with some other players as Buddy looked out at them from his bed and explained how he could no longer brush his teeth. McCarney remembers, "There were tears rolling down his face."

Had Buddy retained the use of his hands, Rosemarie is certain he would have been better able to cope, and that perhaps he would never have contemplated suicide. But given the scope of his injury, the possibility of doing just that would rely on the help of someone else, just as eating and bathing and other aspects of his daily life did. Guy Driesbach remembers that he dropped by one day and found Buddy "really low." Buddy asked, "Guy, go get those pills over there and give me the whole bottle." But Driesbach could not bring himself to do it, just as Brian Sheehan could not bring himself to comply when Buddy pleaded, "Brian, you've got to help me out of this." I remember hearing from one woman years later who said that Buddy asked her to come into the house and leave the gas on in the oven. And there were others. But no one would lend him a hand to help him die—how could they? Sadly, they told him, *Buddy, I could never live with myself.* Or, *Jeez, Buddy I could go to jail.* Or, *It would kill your mother if you did something like that.* Quickly, Buddy would always say, "Sure, I understand. Okay. No problem." And he would change the subject. Mary Jane Williams remembers, "Buddy used to say, 'Can you believe this? I have to have someone to help me even to kill myself.'" To which Mary Jane replied, "Stop talking like that, Buddy."

It was hard for anyone to know how serious he was, or if he was just offhandedly trying on the idea—to hear himself utter words that would once have seemed unimaginable to him. Until the final few years, quite possibly the latter was so, that only when he began wearing down did he begin shaping his plans. Suicide was against his religion—he understood that—yet that became less of a consideration as the pain swept over him, pain not just physical but born of his continuous dependency. For years, his mother had seen to his every need, cheerfully and without objection. But the stress of doing so had aged her, and she was now breaking down before his eyes—and, due to the osteoporosis, shrinking in size over the years by five inches. Buddy would look at her and think, *What kind of a life is this for her?* It saddened him, how she had been chained to his care and how that had deprived her of even the small pleasures that life had to offer. Driesbach, Sheehan, and others had assured him, "Buddy, your mom is okay with this." Rosemarie had told him the same, again and again, "Buddy, stop worrying!" But Buddy was overcome with guilt, which became even more acute whenever he had to summon her in the middle of the night to assist him with something. He would think, *The poor woman has not had a full eight hours of sleep since I got hurt.*

From his room Buddy cried, "Mom! Mom!"

Rosemarie was in the back bedroom by herself, her fractured bones supported by a brace. Gingerly, she got out of bed and padded down the hallway, gathering what she could of the good humor she always had on display for Buddy.

"What is it, honey?"

"I hate to bother you, I hate to bother you," said Buddy, his voice cracking with anguish. "But I had a bug on my face."

An insect with wings had landed on his forehead. Rosemarie shooed it.

"Mom, I am so sorry," Buddy said, tears in his eyes. "I am so, so sorry."

Rosemarie smiled at him. "Oh, Buddy, it's okay. I'm fine."

Whom would he turn to when she was gone? She had asked me that question when I had visited them that Sunday, but he had been pondering it himself with some dismay: What would happen to him when she was no longer there to take care of him? Given how he and Bert got along, the inexplicable chasm between them, Buddy could not conceive of relying on him for his care. Patti and Rudy . . . possibly; Patti would later say that she and her husband had spoken of building an addition to take Buddy in. But Buddy was troubled by the idea of imposing on any of his siblings, even if they would surely have pulled together somehow and come to his aid. As he assessed his options, he wondered, if he lived long enough, would he end up warehoused in some long-term-care facility? The possibility of that horrified him. He remembered the experience he had had years before at the local rehabilitation hospital, where he would say that the staff had ignored him to the point where he had become dehydrated. Is that what he could look forward to when "Saint" Rosemarie died?

But it was not just what would happen to him that would weigh so decisively in his thinking. Of greater consequence was that, by relieving her of her burden as caretaker, he could give his mother a few years of freedom, of going out with her friends for lunch and not having to hurry back for him. Exactly how he would accomplish that would be an elaborate puzzle, especially if he needed the help of the strange character from Michigan who seemed to be on every news channel. How would he get in touch with someone like that? Did Kevorkian even have a phone number you could call? Or did you have to know someone who knew him? And how would he get to Michigan? Somebody would have to fly out there with him, someone he could trust to keep his plan from his mother, who would, Buddy knew, never let him out the door if she found out about it.

Whom could he go to with this?

There was only one person he could be sure of: Jimmy.

. . . . .

Jimmy, after his crash.

. . . . .

SIXTEEN

The Lion and the Mouse

Jimmy spotted her sitting by the pool table at Kelly's Bar in Doylestown. There with a friend, he was kidding around, just as he always did, when he asked Lisa Lepri if she would like to play. Lisa, an attractive young woman with long hair and a sweet smile, picked up a cue and began whipping Jimmy in eight-ball. He would remember how embarrassing it was; no girl had ever beaten him in anything. But Jimmy was working with a handicap: eight years had passed and he had yet to fully recover from the automobile accident. His vision was still blurred. Whenever he lined up a shot, his hand would begin to shake, and the cue ball would veer off course. They played for a while, an hour or so, had a few beers, and by the end of the evening they had exchanged telephone numbers.

Lisa lived upstairs from a Woolworth in a small place that looked out on Main Street. She was divorced and on her own, supporting herself as a sales representative. When Jimmy called her, they went out to dinner, then back to the room he occupied in the basement. They sat up and talked. Jimmy explained what had happened to

Buddy and what had happened to him, how he had once had a chance to play baseball professionally but had become so homesick that he had sabotaged himself. Then there was the crash—again, stupid. Quietly, Lisa looked on as he spoke and could see that he was still a boy trapped at age eleven, that Jimmy had been impaired by his devotion to Buddy. Jimmy could do nothing for him, yet he wanted to do everything. Lisa and Jimmy talked for hours and a friendship began, one that would later become intimate, but only briefly. Lisa would invite him to her apartment, where one evening she handed him an old book with yellow, cracked pages.

"Here," she said as they sat on the edge of her bed, "read from this."

"What is it?"

"A book of fables."

"Fables?"

Lisa smiled. "Read the first one."

He shrugged and turned to it, thinking, *Okay, if this is what turns her on* . . .

" 'The Lion and the Mouse,' " he began, squinting at the print. " 'The lion, tired with the chase, lay sleeping under a shady tree. Some mice that were scrambling over him while he slept awoke him.' "

Jimmy lowered the book and said self-consciously, "What is this?"

"Go on," Lisa said. "Finish it."

Jimmy looked down at the page and continued, " 'Some mice' . . . ah . . . 'Laying his paw upon one of them, he was about to crush him, but the mouse begged for mercy in such moving terms that he let him go. Sometime after, the lion was caught in a net laid by some hunters and unable to free himself. He made the forest resound with his roars. The mouse whose life he had spared came, and his little, sharp teeth gnawed the ropes asunder and set the lion free.' "

Jimmy closed the book and said, "This is crazy."

Nothing would ever be the same for Jimmy after the accident. His once-strapping body had to be held up by a cane. Gone were the physical skills that had come so easily to him: He could no longer run or jump, and even walking up a flight of stairs was a challenge. During his convalescence, when he got out to a high school basketball game, he had to crawl up the steps to the door on his hands and knees. The dumb asses he hung with got a big laugh at his expense; he would always remember that. In the parking lot of a bar one evening, he was beaten in a footrace by a friend who was not only chubby but was running backward. Jimmy says, "It was humiliating." Staring back at him in the bathroom mirror was a face that looked as if it had been caught in a piece of farm machinery: One eye was lower than the other, and a scar on top of his head traveled from ear to ear.

"Lucky, lucky you," Buddy once reminded him. Incredulously, Buddy elaborated, "I play in an innocent football game and look at me: paralyzed. You drink and drive and get into an accident and look at you: up and walking around." Buddy did not say this with any rancor, just bemusement over how capricious destiny could be. Jimmy looked at him, shrugged, and said, "Yeah, I know." But a shadow had now fallen over him, and he began to have an increasingly low opinion of himself. Whatever hope he had once had of resuming his baseball career was now shot, being beyond the reclamation of the physical therapy that he did each day on his own. Even placing a square block into a square hole became a challenge for him. A neuropsychological evaluation performed on him in February 1983 at Temple University Hospital revealed cerebral dysfunction and "a significant drop in overall functioning" from a previous psychological test in 1977. Because Jimmy experienced "potentially disorganized thought processes and difficulty with misinterpretation of situations," the evaluation stated that "he is at risk for behavioral problems." But Jimmy did not have to have a doctor to tell him that something had gone dreadfully wrong inside his head. Years later he would remember that he once asked a friend back then, "Who am I?" Bewildered, the friend looked at him and said, "You're Jim Miley." To which Jimmy replied, "Oh."

In some old home movies that survive from those years, one of a summer picnic is particularly striking: As his parents and siblings and some aunts and uncles socialize, sipping from cups and eating forkfuls of food, Jimmy is off by himself deep in the background, seated at the bottom of a sliding board. A disengaged look is on his face, of being there but not being there . . . of disconnection. While his mother would dote on him and think of him as her baby, and while his brothers and sisters were vigilant in always including him in family functions, Jimmy would come to see himself as an outsider. "Everyone who loved me said, 'Jimmy, you got to get help,'" Jimmy says. But he would not do that for years, and even then he would skip taking his medication, which would leave him vulnerable to mood swings. Early on, he medicated himself by drinking and exhibited odd behavior. Some nights he would emerge from his basement bedroom and begin running through the darkness, his legs still uncertain beneath him as he dodged cars along the highway and the sweat dripped off his face. Jimmy remembers, "I knew how fucked-up I was."

Not knowing what to do or where to go, Jimmy did what generations of American youth had done before him: He bought a van and headed to California. With $1,500 in his pocket, he drove cross-country with an old high school friend and his girlfriend, a stripper from North Jersey. They swung by and picked her up, then doubled back and followed a southern route across the country. They stopped in Arkansas to see a friend, and then their engine overheated in the heart of Texas. While Jimmy and his friends hid in some bushes, their female companion sweet-talked a mechanic into giving them a deal on the repair. From there, it was off to El Paso, where Jimmy looked up an old Little League coach who had settled there, then it was across the Arizona desert to Southern California. Ten days after they had left Pennsylvania, they settled in San Diego in an apartment on Ocean Beach, where each day they walked up the block, stretched out their towels, and lounged in the sand at the foot of the blue Pacific.

None of the jobs that Jimmy eventually found in California lasted more than a week or so. He had one driving an ice cream truck that ended after only a day. Surrounded by swarms of children shouting for his attention, he became confused counting out the change. Eventually, he just pulled over to the side of the road and began eating his wares, a cornucopia of sugary treats that left him too ill to report to work the following day. He remembers having a construction job for a day or so, then he hooked on with a carnival in Palm Springs, where he worked for a week at a stand whipping up Mexican fare. Jimmy says, "I had never even heard of a burrito before." With money running low, he remembers that he and his two friends stopped in a strip club. The girl inquired about a job but did not get it, for reasons that Jimmy can no longer remember. But California was beginning to get old, so when Jimmy found $80 on the street, he wired his brother Bob for the balance of the airfare, said good-bye to his van and his friends, and headed back home to Warminster.

Though he was happy to be home again, he had to admit that it had been good to get away. Even when he was in Florida playing baseball, as saddened as he had been on certain days to be down there instead of with Buddy, a part of him was drawn by the freedom that came with being on his own. No one was calling upon him to help out with chores: "It was always 'Jimmy, I need a drink.' 'Jimmy, give me the phone.' 'Can you scratch my nose?' 'Can you exercise my legs?' 'Can you fix my piss bag?' Jimmy, Jimmy, Jimmy." Even with his head wrapped with bandages at Temple University Hospital, he enjoyed the relative peace that came with the solitude of his convalescence. But in Florida and in the hospital and in California, whatever relief he enjoyed would only be ephemeral, swept away by the same unrelenting guilt that used to overcome him when his injuries had healed enough to allow him to begin walking and then running again. It pained him to think that he would get better and not Buddy. Eventually, Jimmy began running at the high school track instead of in the neighborhood. Jimmy remembers, "Running in the neighborhood, I knew that he could see me when I passed by his window."

Recovery came in baby steps over years and only with the help of Lisa, of whom Jimmy says, "She got me out of the basement." Until she got him to open up to her, he had been unsure of himself and easily confused. When he came back from California, he got back his old job delivering medical supplies, only to discover that he could not remember how to get to the addresses where he was supposed to drop off his packages. In the summers he worked on a landscaping crew; as he remembers, "I began as a weed-whacker and worked up to cutting grass." In the winter he shoveled snow, but only briefly. He says, "Eighteen inches were piled up the day I went out, and I said, 'Screw this!'" Evenings were spent upstairs with Buddy, where they would watch TV or talk sports, or down in the basement by himself doing physical therapy. Jimmy says, "Basically, I was a zombie." But Lisa identified palpable signs of life amid the wreckage, an appealing good-heartedness and depth of feeling that belied the party-animal image he had portrayed. Lisa remembers, "But he was just kind of all over the place, a shell of what he could be."

They moved in together, but not at her apartment and not in the basement. By virtue of some savings that Buddy had scraped together from some successful beef-and-beers, he had purchased a three-bedroom house up the street with a young woman he befriended.

Buddy had hoped that the two of them would move in together and he could thus assert his independence, but according to his brother Bob, the woman ended the relationship because of an "inability to deal with the wheelchair." While not surprising to Buddy, it was a blow to him—another one. With the house up for sale in the wake of the breakup, Buddy convinced Bob to buy it so Jimmy would have a place to live. Jimmy did not earn enough to pay the rent, but Lisa told him she would give up her apartment and share the expenses with him. Only then did Lisa gain full understanding of just how connected Buddy and Jimmy were, how fraught the relationship had been with camaraderie, anger, honesty, and deep, deep love. Jimmy says with a laugh, "People would wonder why I did not have a girlfriend. Ha! Buddy was my girlfriend."

Jimmy was always there to lend a hand. Given his uncertain moods, it would piss him off on some days to be called upon to do something for Buddy. But he kept it to himself—or tried to—and played the clown again, laugh, laugh, and laugh until Buddy would laugh along. Or until Buddy would become aggravated with him and chase him home. Only later would he vent the frustrations that welled up in him. Lisa would hear him pound on the speed bag suspended in the corner of his bedroom. Jimmy would slap it as hard as he could, again and again, as if by beating it he could settle an old score, square an overdue account. Lisa says, "Buddy and Jimmy were so intertwined. I used to think that if Buddy had a pain, then Jimmy had a pain. It was an understanding they had."

Because of that understanding, Buddy knew that Jimmy would be the only one who could help free him from his quandary. No one could appreciate better than Jimmy what Buddy had gone through, the pain he was in, because Jimmy himself had experienced it, even if only to a lesser degree. Jimmy knew what it had been like to have a fine, superbly conditioned young body and to have it become broken.

He knew as no one else did what it was like to look up from a hospital bed at the ceiling and wonder what his body would still be able to do. Buddy would not have to explain any of this to Jimmy. Only he had a sense of what Buddy had endured, because Jimmy had endured it himself. And he remembered what it was like to be so completely helpless.

. . . . .

*Buddy with Karen prior to Yvonne and Glenn
Davis' wedding reception, 1996.*

·····

SEVENTEEN

Alabama Karen

O n their way home that July evening in 1996, they ended up impossibly lost. Strapped in his wheelchair in the back of the old van, which always seemed to be on the verge of tipping over and took forever to work up any speed even with the accelerator to the floor, Buddy had told Karen not to worry, that he knew where he was going. But one wrong turn led to another, and then another, and before long she had steered them into a run-down section of Philadelphia, where they looked conspicuously out of place—Buddy in a tuxedo and Karen in an ankle-length, black dress. In search of a freeway—any freeway—Karen sat behind the wheel with her high heels on her lap in case some unsavory character approached the van at a stoplight. Buddy seemed to think they would work well as impromptu weapons.

"I've never hit anyone in my life," Karen told him. "You just may be on your own here."

"Wouldn't you defend me?"

"Sure I would, after I stopped crying."

"Tell 'em you're just taking your crazy husband out for a nice evening," Buddy said. "If that doesn't work, hit 'em in the face with your shoes."

"How about I just drive off?"

"In this thing? They'd catch us."

"Better yet, how about we look for a 7-Eleven and I run in and get directions?"

Buddy grinned and told her, "You look beautiful tonight."

It had been just over a year since he had gotten back in touch with her. They had not spoken in six years or more. She wondered what had become of him, if he was even still alive. Oddly, she had been thinking of him off and on for weeks when one day she received a telephone call at the University of Alabama Birmingham Hospital, where she worked as a registered nurse in the Adult Cardiac Catheterization Laboratory. On the other end of the line was a man who identified himself as a private investigator from Pennsylvania. He told her he was calling on behalf of his client Buddy Miley and asked for permission to give Buddy her number. Karen remembers, "He said if it was something I was uncomfortable with, he would just tell Buddy he had not been able to reach me." Surprised yet intrigued, Karen told the caller to give Buddy her home number, that she was frequently too busy at work to take personal calls. Buddy called her the following evening.

Eleven years had passed since she had left Warminster and gone back to Florida. While they had occasionally spoken after she and Jessica had moved out on their own—only two or three times—he had faded from her life as if he were a far-off radio signal. Because she had told him so—if only to prevent him from hearing it secondhand—he knew that she was now remarried. Within weeks of returning to Florida in the fall of 1983, she had become acquainted with Ron Kollmeyer, then a respiratory therapist at Largo Medical Center.

They began dating the following January and less than a year later were wed in a small ceremony. Ron reminded Karen in appearance of the actor Tom Selleck and, as she would look back on it years later, provided her with a stability that had been lacking in her life. They had a son, Cory. Ron moved on to a better-paying sales position in Alabama with a medical technology company, Medtronic. He and Karen settled in with their two children in a four-bedroom house in suburban Birmingham that overlooked a serene lake.

Hearing from Buddy again would eventually stir up some old apprehensions in Karen. Initially, he had seemed upbeat, free of the yearning that had always enveloped him years before. "God," he told her, "you sound great!" Karen remembers a cheerful, what-have-you-been-up-to? conversation, one she was pleased to have. When it was over, Buddy asked if he could call again. Karen told him yes, of course, reassured by the strength she sensed in his voice that he now occupied a better place. But when she heard from him again a few days later at work and then on several other occasions, she began to perceive an edge in his voice and began to wonder, *Why is he calling?* Fear was in his voice, and it seemed to well up from a place that was flooded with dread: Mom was falling apart. What would happen to him if she died? Where would he go? "The picture he painted was a bleak one," Karen says. But not until Buddy asked her if she would help set him up in an apartment in Birmingham did she realize just how distressed Buddy had become.

"Are you kidding me?" Karen asked.

"You would only have to drop by and see me once a month or so," Buddy told her. "I know you have a life and I would not interfere with it."

Karen replied, "Buddy, what are you thinking? How do you even think that would work?"

Buddy relented. "Yeah, I guess it was a bad idea."

Buddy would not bring it up again. But in their very next conversation, a day or so later, he broached the subject that Karen would say had been his plan B: Kevorkian. He called Karen at work and asked if she knew how he could get in contact with him. Stunned, Karen said, "What?" Buddy explained that he just assumed that since she worked in a hospital, one of the doctors she worked with would have a telephone number for him. Not knowing exactly what to say, Karen told Buddy she was in no position to talk just then, that he should call her later that evening at home. When Buddy did, Karen immediately asked, "Does this have to do with me not wanting you to come down here to live?" Buddy assured her that it did not and told her he had been thinking of ending his life for years. Karen would wonder.

Unequivocally, Karen told him she would not help him contact Kevorkian—however one did that. Buddy would have to do this on his own, and she questioned if he would be able to do it. Karen says, "I remember thinking it was like if you have a teenager who asks for a tattoo and you tell him, 'Okay, but only if you earn enough to pay for it.' And that becomes the end of it." But she told Buddy he could rely on her for support—that he could call her to talk it over. Buddy told her he understood. He said she would be the only person he would share any of this with and added pointedly, "Mom can never know. It would kill her." When weeks then passed and not another word was said on the subject, Karen just assumed that he had not followed through or had encountered some other obstacle. But one day in the fall of 1995, Buddy surprised her when he told her that he had contacted Kevorkian, or, to be precise, one of his associates. From that point on, Buddy apprised of her of developments as the process unfolded, step by step, until she came to understand the following spring that "it was a done deal." Karen says, "All that remained was for them to agree upon a date."

As convincingly as Buddy portrayed his intentions, Karen remembers that a voice inside her whispered, *You could stop this.* But how? It
had been crazy to think he could come down to Alabama—he had to
know that—yet even if the issue appeared resolved between them, that
it had even been addressed seemed to leave it in play in some unspoken
form: *All you have to do is say the word, Karen.* But during their conversations, Karen steered Buddy toward more measured alternatives.
Since he seemed to call her whenever he became especially depressed
or was in intense pain, she asked him if he had been taking any medication for depression or pain. Buddy told her he had, but neither had
worked, and they had only left him disoriented. "It was a conversation
we had frequently," Karen says. "It was not something I just dropped."
Karen wondered if she should pick up the phone and call his mother—
let her in on what Buddy was thinking. With children of her own,
would that not be something she would want someone to do for her?
But Karen told herself that Buddy was an adult, had free will, and had
suffered so terribly long.

Somewhere during this period, they slipped back into a place
they had once occupied so long ago. Karen became to Buddy not a
woman with a husband, two children, and a career in Alabama, but
a disembodied voice that reminded him again of the promise life
once held. While it was not something he could have in fact, it sat
squarely in his imagination and played there for years and years,
every day. Karen . . . if only. Sometimes he would call her at work
just to say, "Good morning." In the evening when he called at her
home, their hour-or-more conversations would stray into an alter-
nate reality, as Buddy would describe the day they had had together.
Karen let it go, even as she knew that as Buddy became playful, she
had crossed some line of propriety. Yet she could not bring herself to
stop him, not with the end so close at hand. How could she deny him
such a small piece of her heart, this sweet man who had suddenly

stepped back into her life from what seemed to be an eternity ago and who was now virtually on his deathbed? She told herself, perhaps wishfully, *Ron will understand.*

Karen had told Ron about Buddy: that he had been paralyzed in a football game and that he had been her high school boyfriend. Ron spoke to him once, and then only briefly—one evening he picked up the phone and Buddy asked him in a soft voice, "Is Karen there?" Karen explained to Ron that Buddy was "going through a tough time." Initially, Ron empathized with her. "I put myself in her position," he says. "What if I had a high school girlfriend that had had something like that happen to her?" But he could sense that the conversations were beginning to wear on Karen, that she had become withdrawn and agitated. Ron remembers that he asked her what was going on, but when she was unresponsive, he did not ask again. Ron says, "I am not a confrontational person, so I would let it go." Ron would be startled to learn from Karen that Buddy had asked to come to Birmingham and that he was scheduling an appointment with Kevorkian. But Karen did not share the personal aspects of her conversations with Buddy, and Ron appeared content to remain on the periphery of what he perceived to be an act of compassion by his wife. Of the affection Buddy had for Karen, Ron says, "I guess she was his last good memory."

Ron gave his blessing when Karen told him she would like to go up to see Buddy and say good-bye. "I understood it was something she needed to do," he says. "My thinking was, 'She has to do something to work this out.'" Karen scheduled two weeks of vacation from work. Ron booked her airline reservations and dropped her off at Birmingham International Airport. Five hours or so later, with a stop in Atlanta, she stepped off her plane in Philadelphia and there was Buddy, along with a friend who had driven him. Even under the circumstances—or perhaps even because of them—Buddy was ecstatic to see her, so giddy that he even told the skycap that she was his wife and that he had not seen her in ten years! Again, Karen let it go, thinking, *Let him have his fun.* It was off then to Warminster. The house was just as she remembered it from years ago. Rosemarie greeted her warmly, yet she wondered what Karen was doing there. It had been so long. Offhandedly, Rosemarie asked her at one point during her stay, "What does your husband think of this?" Cheerfully, Karen said he was fine with it, that he knew she and Buddy were just old friends.

Quickly, Buddy and Karen fell into stride again as if just days and not years had separated them. "We just hung out," Karen says. Every day they went outside or they did some errands. Buddy would ask her, "Pull over and get out. I love to see you walk." In the evenings they would talk. Only briefly did the subject of Kevorkian come up, yet Karen remembers they did debate the afterlife. Karen says, "I tried to get him to have some imagination about it." Karen shared her views on reincarnation, that we are sent here to learn how to love and that whatever lessons remain unlearned at our passing, we are given another chance to grasp them in a subsequent life. Buddy just laughed. "Nah," he countered, ever the Catholic boy. "You live, you die. You go to heaven. You go to hell." But Karen remembers that the levity that Buddy affected had an edge to it. "Buddy knew it was suicide and he knew it was against his religion," Karen says. "But he believed that the suffering he had endured was so immense that there was no way that God would deny him heaven."

It had been a lovely trip.

So . . . effortless.

Karen remembers, "I knew it was going to kill him when I left."

Yet the inevitable was averted.

Buddy told her he had been invited to a wedding reception in July. Yvonne Ameche would be marrying another Heisman Trophy winner, Glenn Davis, who'd starred at West Point as the legendary "Mr. Outside" with fellow running back Doc Blanchard ("Mr. Inside"). Buddy and Yvonne had grown even closer since the Heisman ball had been stolen. With tears in her eyes, Yvonne had called him with the news of what had happened. But Buddy told her, "As long as you're okay, nothing else matters." Yvonne had met Davis, a widower, at a Heisman party the year before and one day brought him by the house to see Buddy. Yvonne told him, "Glenn, you sit and tell Buddy how you once dated Liz Taylor, while Rosemarie and I go in the other room and have coffee." Davis had indeed dated the stunning young starlet during his bachelor days in Los Angeles. As Davis and Yvonne were preparing to leave, Buddy warned him, "You better take care of her. I may be Irish, but I know people on the outside." Buddy told Karen he would not attend the wedding reception unless she went with him.

"Come on, Karen," he said. "Just think of it like the prom we never had a chance to attend."

She could not say no. "Okay, Buddy. I think I can do that."

Ron was perplexed when Karen told him she was planning a second trip to Warminster. Realizing that "nothing had been resolved," that the stress on her was just continuing to build, he told her, "You need to put an end to this." But Ron did not stand in her way, and Karen came back up for a long weekend in early July. Karen says, "I was going to let him have whatever fantasy he wanted. It was the last dance." On the day of the event, Buddy was helped into his tux, accessories, and shoes. Patti groomed his hair and, at the behest of Buddy, did Karen up in a French twist. At the posh Aronimink Golf Club, which on this evening was overflowing with football royalty, Karen wheeled Buddy into the reception, where they remained by the door as Buddy chatted with some other guests. Always, he introduced Karen and explained who she was—and who she should have been. Again, Karen let it go. Only there for just over an hour, they did stay long enough to greet Yvonne and for someone to snap a photograph of the two of them: Buddy and Karen, the way it was supposed to be.

Getting home that evening was long and scary but a thoroughly amusing trip, full of just living in the here and now. Rosemarie was up waiting for them when they got back, and Jimmy was called to help bone-weary Buddy out of his tux and into bed. Not until two days later—Monday—did the sudden realization set in that Karen would be leaving—this time for good. But that was how it always was: Whatever sadness there would be between them would always be held off until the end. Buddy told her, "I will never see you again. Can you believe that?" Softly Karen replied, "I know."

Had a passerby glanced at them at her gate at the airport on the day of her departure, he or she would perhaps have looked away to afford them some small privacy. Buddy sat in his wheelchair with Karen on his lap. The friend who had driven them to the airport had walked off. Tears streamed from their eyes as they searched for the words to say good-bye. They became so preoccupied that Karen did not see the other passengers begin to board, and she did not hear the final call for her flight. Only when she looked up and saw that the door to the Jetway had been closed did she jump up and say, "Oh, God! I gotta go!" But the gate attendant would not open the door for her. It was against federal regulations. So Karen stood by the window and looked out: There was her plane, and it would be leaving without her.

Jimmy's note.

EIGHTEEN

Brothers

Jimmy stood at the end of the hallway with a putter in his hands. With his head down, he eyed the golf ball sitting at his feet and then tapped it. It picked up speed as it rolled over the rug and swerved toward the automatic return cup, which he had picked up during a move. Possessions had come to him in this way, and that was even how he had furnished his house. The sofa and the table and chairs had been left behind by customers, still-usable pieces that, while threadbare or scratched, were among the few bonuses that came from working your ass off on a moving van. Given that he had taken up golf, Jimmy was thrilled when he looked in a pile of discarded belongings one day and found that 19th Hole Electric Putting Cup.

Cooper stood off to the side as the ball Jimmy putted skidded and bounced over the rug. Cooper, whose first name was Mark but who was known by everyone as just Cooper, had played sports with Jimmy through school. They became close friends as the years unfolded, often speaking on the phone several times a day. At a glance, they appeared an unlikely pair: Jimmy looked as if he just stepped off the cover of a surfer magazine, and Cooper, black, five feet six, and 290 pounds, had the appearance of a large oval. Jimmy would come to him for advice, and Cooper dispensed it so freely that Rosemarie would come to affectionately call him "Cooper the psychiatrist." The owner of a small limousine service, he would drop by to see Jimmy if business was slow, and they would shoot the breeze.

The ball slid into the cup and popped out.

Jimmy raked it back with his club.

Not looking up, he asked, "Did you ever hear of Dr. Jack Kevorkian?"

Cooper squinted. "Kevorkian? Oh, yeah. Yeah. The guy with the suicide thing."

"Well, Buddy wants to go to him. And he wants me to take him. What do you think?"

Cooper did not know what to say, not immediately. Finally he said, "I don't know, Jim. If it was my brother? I couldn't do it. And I couldn't see doing something like that myself."

Jimmy looked down and tapped the ball back at the cup. He looked back up at Cooper. "Buddy is in a lot of pain, and this is his decision. I want to give him his wish, you know? More than anything."

Cooper sighed. "That's your opinion. But I'm kind of against it."

Jimmy shrugged. "Yeah, I know. The whole thing's fucked-up."

What Jimmy remembers is that it came together in seven months. From August 1996 until the following March, he found himself drawn into a whirlpool of colliding emotions, of knowing what he had to do but not always sure that he should do it. For years, he had prayed, *God, let him get better. Please. Please.* But it was not going to happen, and he had to let go of the idea that it ever would. Unaware of how long Buddy had been discussing his plans with Karen—and how intent he had been in those conversations—Jimmy wondered when Buddy asked him to take him to Kevorkian if it was just talk. He had hoped that it was, that he would be spared having to decide what to do. Suicide was not an easy subject for him to ponder. But there was a day that summer Jimmy would look back on and think of as a tipping point.

Patti had come over to the house that day, as she always did, and she and Jimmy wheeled Buddy out into the sun. They positioned Buddy on his back on a chiropractic table that they had set up. The warm rays fell on his pale skin. Jimmy and Patti then turned him over on his stomach and discovered a red bedsore on his lower back the size of a quarter. They glanced at each other and cringed: *Oh, no, not this again.* Buddy had battled them on and off for years. Always, they began small but grew larger. Sensing that he had another one, Buddy asked, "Is it bad?" Quietly, Jimmy just looked at him and said, "Pretty bad."

Jimmy thought then, *This is just no way to live.*

But he was still not sure.

He had questions.

Years ago, all Buddy would have had to do was utter the word *orange* and his command would have been followed. But they were no longer boys. As he and Buddy talked it over, Jimmy found that the questions seemed to rush at him at once. Eyes ablaze with uncertainty, he asked Buddy how this was going to work, what he had to do, if he would get into any trouble. Calmly, Buddy looked out at him from his wheelchair and told him that they would fly to Michigan and that it would be done there in a hotel room. Buddy told him Jimmy would be fine. But he was not so sure . . . he had to think. Mom . . . what would she think? What would everybody think? Buddy told him not to worry, that it would be hard on Mom but she could live her life again.

But Jimmy was still not sure . . . what would people think . . . the neighbors? Buddy looked at him and said, "Screw the neighbors." Jimmy paused and then called to the other room.

"Mom, who's smarter? Me or Buddy?"

From the kitchen, Rosemarie shouted back, "Buddy!"

Jimmy remembers, "I knew what she was going to say. I just had to hear her say it. I guess I thought, 'Okay, I got that answered.' Because if I was smarter, he wasn't going."

Psychologically, Buddy began to slip again that summer. Friends could see it, how exhausted he had become. Part of that had to do with the departure of Karen, who had given him something to look forward to when she came back for the wedding reception. But whenever she would leave through the years, he would become melancholy. It worried his family when this happened, which is why Buddy would become so secretive in letting anyone know he was talking to or corresponding with her. Karen remembers that Vinnie the mailman would send back the photographs of her and her children once Buddy had a chance to see them. In the conversations that Karen had with Buddy once she got back to Alabama, she remembers that he indeed became dispirited, that she could sense the struggle in his voice. But she would not learn of an episode that occurred one evening when he came back from visiting with a friend a few doors away.

Often, Buddy would go up to visit Mary Jane Williams and her family, who lived no more than a hundred yards away on Acorn Drive. On this evening, Buddy had just gotten an electric wheelchair. Mary Jane accompanied him back to her house, but at the end of the visit Buddy told her he would get home on his own. Well acquainted with how despondent Buddy had become, Mary Jane stood at the end of her driveway and looked on as Buddy proceeded down the street, led by a bouncing beam of light from his flashlight. But Buddy did not turn for home. Instead, he crossed the intersection at Acorn and Kingsley. Mary Jane hurried inside and in a panic called the Mileys, certain that Buddy was heading up to County Line Road to drive into traffic. When his father picked up the phone, Mary Jane exclaimed, "Mr. Miley, Buddy just went past your house in the wheelchair." Bert ran out the door and found his son on the ground, crying. The wheelchair had gotten caught in the grass and had toppled over. Bert told Mary Jane as she arrived on the scene, "Don't worry. It'll be all right. I'll take care of it." Mary Jane remembers, "Buddy was angry, embarrassed, and frustrated—every word you can think of. He just wanted to die."

Jimmy finally told Buddy he would do it, yet Buddy was concerned—not just if Jimmy would follow through, but about the effect it would have on his erratic and fragile brother. Consequently, Buddy would ask others if they could take him. When he posed the question to Rudy, who had wheeled him out on South Beach just a few years before, his brother-in-law told him gently, "Buddy, that would be a lot to ask of me. I love you, but I would not be able to live with myself." Buddy told him he understood. He later summoned George Bushman to the house and asked him. Bushman told him the only way he would do it is if Buddy cleared it with Rosemarie. Buddy stopped him and said, "Okay. Forget it." Buddy did not ask anyone else, but he did let them know what he had planned, people including Yvonne, Dave Heilbrun, and a handful of others he could trust to keep his intentions secret. According to Heilbrun, the United Airlines pilot who years before had built the addition, what Buddy was asking Jimmy to do weighed on Buddy. Heilbrun remembers, "Right off the bat, I think he thought Jim would do it. But he knew that it would upset him."

Some years later a note was found attached to a scrapbook that Buddy left behind. It appeared to have been written by Jimmy and said simply, *Buddy, I'll get you there*. Jimmy has no recollection of having written it, but then he had only a vague recollection of the part he played in the months leading up to their departure. He did find a telephone number for Kevorkian and gave it to Buddy, who told him to slip it into a book by his bed. Jimmy conceded that, given what Karen had been privy to, Buddy could well have been in contact with Kevorkian by then. Jimmy remembers Buddy asking him to get his medical records and send them to an address he had for Kevorkian in Michigan. To better explain his ordeal—and perhaps seal the deal—Buddy asked Jimmy to include a copy of the article I had written three years before: "19 Years of Hell." Jimmy remembers that whenever he dropped by the house, Buddy told him to take a piece of memorabilia home with him. Buddy would ask, "What do you want?" Jimmy would say, "Nothing." But Buddy would insist and Jimmy would leave with something under his arm.

Outwardly, Jimmy appeared to be calm as the preparations unfolded. Other than Cooper and a few others, the only person Jimmy confided in was Lisa, who had moved out of his house in early November. When Jimmy told her what Buddy had planned—and she had assured herself by speaking with Buddy that it was indeed what he wanted to do—Lisa told Jimmy, "Let me know if you would like me to come along." But Jimmy told her he would be fine. Perhaps he even believed that himself when he said it, or perhaps it had not yet become real to him. Even in conversations with the psychiatrist he had started seeing in November 1994 for cognitive problems, the subject had not been a focal point of any of his sessions. According to Timothy J. Michals, M.D., P.C., Jimmy did not even bring up Kevorkian until their December 23, 1996, appointment. Even then, he did it in an offhand, by-the-way manner at the end of their hour. He had been more concerned that day whether his psychological condition would prevent him from obtaining a license to drive commercial vehicles. Michals says, "It came out as an addendum, an explosion at the end of the session. Jimmy said, 'My brother is talking about going to Dr. Kevorkian and I am supposed to be taking him.' "

But Jimmy was somewhat less composed than he appeared. Buddy had a lot of friends—how could Jimmy ever look any of them in the eye again? And what would Mom say? Or Patti or Linda or Rose or Joanne or Bob? Buddy had approached the subject of suicide with Bob in December, and he had become outraged by the very mention of it. Dad . . . whoever knew what he was thinking? Jimmy reminded Buddy in one of their conversations, "This is not like Lourdes. You are not coming back from this. This is final." Buddy told him he knew that. To settle the anxiety that was churning inside him, Jimmy began to think of how he used to gear up for a game. He told himself, *Get your head together.* But it had become hard to do that because they could not seem to arrive at a firm date. They had one, but Kevorkian needed to cancel. Jimmy remembers feeling relieved. They arranged a second one, and Buddy had to cancel because of the death of Uncle Frankie. Jimmy became agitated. He told Buddy, "If you have to cancel again, get somebody else." Jimmy remembers, " 'Cause it was too hard for me. He knew."

Quietly, word of what was afoot spread through the family. Buddy spoke with his sister Linda in January 1997 and told her what he planned to do, saying, "I've had enough." Linda replied, "Bud, I totally get it." One evening in early February, Linda and her husband, Mike, invited Rose, Joanne, Patti, and Rudy over to her house to discuss the situation. Neither Jimmy nor Bob was asked to be there: Jimmy, because of what it appeared he had been chosen to do; and Bob, because he had been so opposed to the idea when Buddy had proposed it. The siblings talked about how, when it happened, they would break the news to their parents. They wondered if Jimmy would be able to do it, or if taking Buddy to Michigan would send him spiraling into even deeper emotional problems. But no one in the room had an alternative, and surely none could see themselves doing it. So it would have to be Jimmy: little Jimmy, the silly boy who so long ago they had hung up on a coat hanger in the closet. Of anyone they could think of back then and even later, he would have been the last person they could imagine being given such a grave assignment. But they had to agree: No one had loved a brother any more.

Two weeks before the appointment with Kevorkian, a funeral was held for Uncle Frankie. Largely, he had had a happy life, even with the hardship with which he had come into the world sixty-seven years before. Coldly told so long ago by the nurse at the hospital, "Take the idiot home," Nana had cradled her Down syndrome boy in her arms and would forever shelter him from the cruelty of strangers. When in old age she was forced to sell her house, it had wounded her to think that Frankie would have to leave her side and go into a home. Sadly, Nana told her daughter Rosemarie, with whom she had gone to live, "I never thought it would come to this." Ever cheerful, Frankie would outlive her and spend ten years cared for by professionals, until one day his body began to break down. With his prognosis poor, his doctors asked Rosemarie and her three other brothers, "How much more do you want to put him through?"

So they let him go.

Jimmy attended the services at St. Helena Church in North Philadelphia. Although he had always been fond of Frankie—just as everyone had been—he had not expected to be seized by the outpouring of grief that he experienced during the service. Standing in a pew with him, his family eyed him curiously, not sure exactly what to think. But Jimmy would come to realize that the tears he shed that day were not for poor Frankie, but for what was to come in just two more weeks.

Jimmy thought, *There's going to be another funeral soon. And it'll be because of me.*

. . . . .

STATE OF MICHIGAN
DEPARTMENT OF PUBLIC HEALTH

CERTIFICATE OF DEATH

LF 000324
CF

STATE FILE NUMBER
1192867

1. DECEDENT'S NAME (First Middle Last)	2. SEX	3. DATE OF DEATH (Month Day Year)
Albert G. Miley, Jr.	Male	Mar 19, 1997

4a. AGE - Last Birthday (Years)	4b. UNDER 1 YEAR MONTHS DAYS	4c. UNDER 1 DAY HOURS MINUTES	5. DATE OF BIRTH (Month Day Year)	6. COUNTY OF DEATH
41			January 28, 1956	Wayne

7a. LOCATION OF DEATH (Enter place officially pronounced dead in 7a, 7b, 7c)
QUALTIY INN RM #146

7b. IF HOSP or INST Inpatient, Op./Emer., Room, DOA (Specify)

7c. CITY, VILLAGE or TOWNSHIP OF DEATH
Livonia

8. SOCIAL SECURITY NUMBER	9a. USUAL OCCUPATION	9b. KIND OF BUSINESS OR INDUSTRY
177-50-8023	Never Employed	

10a. CURRENT RESIDENCE - STATE	10b. COUNTY	10c. LOCALITY	10d. STREET AND NUMBER
Pennsylvania	Bucks	TWP OF Warminster	120 Acorn Drive

10e. ZIP CODE	11. BIRTHPLACE (City and State or Foreign Country)	12. MARITAL STATUS	13. SURVIVING SPOUSE	14. WAS DECEDENT EVER IN U.S. ARMED FORCES?
18974	Philadelphia, PA	Never Married		No

15. ANCESTRY	16. RACE	17. DECEDENT'S EDUCATION Elementary/Secondary (0-12)
American	White	12

18. FATHER'S NAME (First Middle Last)	19. MOTHER'S NAME (First Middle Surname before first marriage)
Albert G. Miley	Rosemarie Quinn

20a. INFORMANT'S NAME (Type/Print)	20b. MAILING ADDRESS
Rosemarie Miley	120 Acorn Drive, Warminster, Pennsylvania 18974

21. METHOD OF DISPOSITION	22a. PLACE OF DISPOSITION	22b. LOCATION - City or Village State
Burial	Holy Sepulchre Cemetery	Cheltenham, Pennsylvania

23. SIGNATURE OF FUNERAL SERVICE LICENSEE	24. LICENSE NUMBER	25. NAME AND ADDRESS OF FACILITY
	6552	McCabe Funeral Home - Canton Chapel, 851 Canton Center Road, Canton, Michigan 48187

26. PART I. Enter the diseases, injuries, or complications that caused the death. Do NOT enter the mode of dying such as cardiac or respiratory arrest, shock, or heart failure. List only one cause on each line.

IMMEDIATE CAUSE → Pending

DUE TO (OR AS A CONSEQUENCE OF):

DUE TO (OR AS A CONSEQUENCE OF):

DUE TO (OR AS A CONSEQUENCE OF):

PART II. Other significant conditions contributing to death but not resulting in the underlying cause given in Part I.

27a. WAS AN AUTOPSY PERFORMED?	27b. WERE AUTOPSY FINDINGS AVAILABLE PRIOR TO COMPLETION OF CAUSE OF DEATH?
Yes	Yes

28. ACTUAL PLACE OF DEATH	29. WAS CASE REFERRED TO MEDICAL EXAMINER?
Hotel	Yes

31a. On the basis of examination and/or investigation, in my opinion death occurred at the time, date and place and due to the cause(s) and manner stated.

(Signature and Title) Cheryl Loewe

30b. DATE SIGNED	31b. DATE SIGNED	31c. CASE NUMBER
	Mar 20, 1997	97-02538

30c. TIME OF DEATH	31d. PRONOUNCED DEAD ON	31e. TIME OF DEATH
M	Mar 19, 1997	9:03am

32a. NAME AND ADDRESS OF PERSON WHO COMPLETED CAUSE OF DEATH	32b. LICENSE NUMBER
Cheryl Loewe, M.D., Asst M.E., 1300 E. Warren, Det. MI 48207	056701

33a. AGE	33b. DATE OF INJURY	33c. TIME OF INJURY	33d. DESCRIBE HOW INJURY OCCURRED
		M	

33e. INJURY AT WORK	33f. PLACE OF INJURY	33g. LOCATION - Street or RFD No.	City	Village or Twp	State

34a. REGISTRAR'S SIGNATURE	34b. DATE FILED (Month Day Year)
Joan McCotter	March 24, 1997

CERTIFICATION

I HEREBY CERTIFY THAT THIS IS A TRUE COPY OF A DEATH CERTIFICATE
ON FILE IN MY OFFICE.

Joan McCotter
JOAN McCOTTER, CITY CLERK
City of Livonia, Wayne County
State of Michigan

DATE MAR 24 1997

Buddy's death certificate.

. . . . .

NINETEEN

Lingering Light

Jimmy turned back an edge of the drapes and looked onto the parking lot at the Quality Inn & Suites in Livonia, Michigan. The contact he had for Kevorkian had asked him to check in and said they would be there once it got dark. Jimmy looked up at the setting sun in the far horizon and quietly wondered, *When does it get dark up here?* He let the drape fall and looked over his shoulder into the room. Buddy was stretched across the top of the bedspread, his wheelchair off to the side. Even with the heat on in the room, Buddy appeared cold, very cold. Lisa got up from her chair along the wall and told Jimmy she was going outside for a cigarette.

When they had gone into the room, Jimmy had looked around: two beds, a TV, and, beyond a door, a bathroom with a tub and shower. It was not the type of room anyone stayed in long, perhaps an overnight or two, or even just an afternoon. Offhandedly, Jimmy tried to imagine the people who had once occupied it, what random events had converged in their lives to draw them here. By any estimate, there had to have been thousands of people who passed through this room—traveling salesmen, truck drivers, or whoever else pulled off the highway in search of affordable accommodations. But Jimmy was fairly sure that whatever else Room 146 had been used for, it had never been the scene of an assisted suicide.

Jimmy glanced at Buddy and told him, "Still light out."

Buddy replied, "It would be dark by now back home."

"You think there is a time change up here?"

"No. Same time zone. It just stays light later."

Jimmy peeked through the drapes again. "Guess so."

Whatever good-byes Buddy had to say had to be handled with discretion during those final two weeks. In some cases, he penned a message on a piece of paper, writing as he always had, with the pen clenched between his teeth. To his brother Bob, he would leave behind a note that was later found in an envelope in his room: SORRY LOVE BUDDY. To his sister Patti, one said, THANKS FOR EVERYTHING, with a VHS copy of a comedy she liked, *The Nutty Professor*. One by one, he would have conversations with each of his siblings that, as they looked back on it, had the feel of a farewell. For his mother, he would leave a voice recording and a teddy bear that he would have delivered to her with a card attached that said: LOVE YOU ALWAYS . . . BUDDY . . . XOXO. But there would be no conciliatory words for his father, nor would there be any recriminations, just more of the silence that had always divided them. In the final few weeks, Buddy arranged to have pictures taken of himself with his nephews and nieces, who had curled up on his chest as babies and whom he had watched play in the yard. One night near the end, Matt, twelve, and Shane, seven, had camped out on his floor in sleeping bags, and Buddy told Rose the following day, "You know, I stayed up all night just staring at them."

With just a few days before he was to leave, he reached out to the friends who had stood by him through the years. Guy Driesbach was traveling when Buddy called and told his wife, "I really need to talk to Guy." Driesbach hurried over to see him that Sunday, at which point Buddy told him, "I have been in touch with Dr. Kevorkian. . . ." Driesbach sat there with tears in his eyes and said, "Whatever you have to do, Bud." Dave Heilbrun told him the same. Calls also went out to Yvonne, who remembers how hollowed out Buddy sounded, and to Pat Delaney, who had been wrapped up in a stressful business deal and let his wife speak with Buddy on the phone. "Do I regret it? . . . Yeah," says Delaney. "He told my wife how much he loved us." Brian Sheehan also spoke with Buddy on Monday evening for over an hour. From the way Buddy sounded—perhaps the way he went to such lengths to thank him—Sheehan got the feeling "something was up." When Sheehan got off the phone, his wife asked, "How is Buddy doing?" Sheehan looked at her and said, "Good. He said good-bye."

And . . . Karen.

The evening before he was to leave, Buddy called her in Alabama. Karen was watching television with Ron and their son, Cory. She had been expecting to hear from Buddy—they had arranged it—yet she was overcome with foreboding, which she tried to dispel by taking a deep breath. For privacy, she slipped down into the basement. Immediately, she could hear how utterly exhausted Buddy sounded, how depleted he had been by the ordeal of these final few days. In what she presumed would be their last conversation, she wondered again if this would even be happening if she had agreed to let him come down there and live. But she did not bring that up. Instead, she told herself that she would let Buddy talk.

And he did.

He told her: Everything was ready. . . . Jimmy would come by in the morning and they would tell Mom that they would be going to the eye doctor. . . . Her health is getting so bad, Karen. I need to get going first so she can still have a life. . . . Jimmy will be fine. I told him I would do this even without him, you know that. I asked him to let you know how everything went. . . .

Buddy paused, his voice breaking. "Oh, God, Karen. Do you know how much I love you? How long I have loved you? I know every inch of your face. I know I would have been a good husband to you. We would have had a good life. I think of that every day."

"Buddy, I . . ."

"Karen, I am so ready. My pain will finally be over. So much pain, so much. I want it to be over. No tears for me, not one. You made my heart full. Remember that. I don't know how to tell you good-bye, so I'm just going to try to sleep now, okay?"

"I've loved you, Buddy. All these years, the best I've known how. . . ."

Then Karen heard a dial tone in her ear.

As the eve of their departure unfolded, Jimmy had been full of worry. He had been increasingly anxious ever since they buried Frankie, which he had kept hidden from even Dr. Michals. In their March 10 session, Jimmy did not refer to the appointment with Kevorkian, years later saying that he feared the doctor would be obligated to report him to the authorities—or so someone had cautioned him. But he did continue to discuss it now and again with Lisa. He finally asked, "I know what I said before, but can you come along?" It had suddenly become "real" to him when he picked up the phone one day at his house and it was Kevorkian, who had wanted to know, "Are you ready?" Jimmy did not know exactly how to answer, so he just said, "I guess so, in a weird way." Lisa drove from the apartment she now had in North Jersey and checked into the Warrington Motor Lodge, where she and Jimmy sat up talking, Jimmy wondering, *What is Buddy thinking?* Jimmy paced the floor. Lisa remembers, "He was like a cat in a cage."

Sleepless, Jimmy got in his car the following morning for the short drive home and suddenly let out a long, anguished cry—what he would later call a "war cry"—*Ahhhhhhhhhhhhh!* Tears spilled down his face as he scolded himself, *Come on, Jim! Pull it together!* What had Buddy told him so long ago, when they were boys playing catch and he had gone crying into the house? "Be a man!" Buddy had told him, for years, but Jimmy always just fooled around, the *"if only* kid" with the face full of freckles. Jimmy told himself, *Well, you better be one now.* He wiped his eyes with his coat sleeve and inhaled a deep breath. Cheerfully, his mother greeted him as he walked through the door and said, "I've done two loads of wash already this morning. What have you done?" Jimmy just looked at her and shrugged, as a voice inside his head screamed, *I'm going to take your son to Dr. Kevorkian today and he's going to die! That's what I've got to do!* Jimmy eyed Buddy and asked, "How are you feeling?" Calmly, Buddy said he was okay, but that they better go. Getting into Center City was always a big hassle. As Jimmy helped Buddy into his coat, Rosemarie leaned over, kissed Buddy on the cheek, and said, "Here . . . for later." She slipped a peanut-butter sandwich into his pocket.

Lisa remembers seeing the van approach as she stood outside her motel. It seemed to be crawling toward her in slow motion. But that was how the whole day would feel to her, as if it were happening at the bottom of the sea. When Lisa got in, she looked back at Buddy. He sat there in his wheelchair passively, as if indeed they were going into Center City to the eye doctor. Jimmy drove carefully, as he always did when Buddy was a passenger. Abrupt stops would cause Buddy pain, so Jimmy eased into stoplights and across intersections. Jimmy guided the van onto the highway and onto the exit for Philadelphia International. Few words were spoken. Jimmy concentrated on the bumper ahead of him with an intensity that reminded him how he used to be whenever he was on a bus going to a game: head up, eyes forward. At the airport, Jimmy parked in the short-term lot, where he helped Buddy from the van and wheeled him inside the terminal.

As the Northwest A320 ascended to a cruising altitude, the three of them settled into the first-class seats to which they had been upgraded. When the flight attendant appeared, Buddy ordered a whiskey and asked for it to be a double. He sipped from the cup as Jimmy held it to his lips. Clouds passed by their window in scattered pieces. Lisa remembers feeling as if they were the only passengers on the plane, and that the journey out to Detroit took not just over an hour but what seemed forever. When they finally landed, Jimmy helped Buddy into his wheelchair and guided him into the terminal. There, Lisa stood with Buddy at a pay phone as he called his sister Linda. Lisa dialed the number and held the receiver up for Buddy to speak. It was 4:00 P.M. or so.

Linda picked up.

Buddy said, "I just called to say good-bye. You know what I'm doing, don't you?"

"Yeah. We figured it out."

"I hope no one is going to be mad at me."

"We're not going to be mad at you," Linda said. "We all understand. And we all love you."

Buddy paused. "Take care of Jimmy."

"Of course, Buddy. Of course we will."

Jimmy got a rental car and they got in: Buddy in the front seat, Lisa in the back. Working from directions he had written down, Jimmy merged onto I-96 and began looking for the signs for Merriman Road. Lisa remembers that the three of them chatted casually, yet a palpable apprehension was in the car. Intently, Jimmy peered over the top of the steering wheel. When he exited at Merriman, Buddy asked him if they could stop at a convenience store. Jimmy asked him what he wanted. Buddy said . . . a comb. The pent-up tension in Jimmy then came rushing out: "A comb? A comb? What do you want a comb for? You're going to be dying in two hours!" Silence then enveloped the car. Jimmy told himself, *Do what he wants! Stop being a dick!* Jimmy spotted a convenience store and pulled into the lot. When he came back out with a comb, Jimmy looked over at Buddy and placed it in his lap. Buddy said nothing.

They went to the hotel. Jimmy went inside to check in, while Buddy and Lisa waited in the car. Jimmy paid for the room in cash— $46—and signed in under the alias of Mike Thomas, the name of a friend back home with whom he had been having some problems. With his room key in hand, Jimmy came back out to the car, where Buddy sat with a pale, depleted look on his face. Lisa remembers that she had held up the cell phone for Buddy to call Karen. The heart-breaking conversation would haunt Karen for years to come. Lisa sat in the back and, as always, tried to give Buddy some privacy and blocked out what was being said. Only Karen would remember that conversation, which she would record in her journal. Jimmy just knew that when it was over, whatever life remained in Buddy appeared to have been drained from him.

Jimmy removed Buddy from the car and placed him into the wheelchair. They went into the room. Buddy asked, "Can you turn on the heat?" Jimmy flipped the switch on the wall and hot air began blowing from the vent. Jimmy helped Buddy out of his wheelchair and arranged him on one of the beds, with his hands folded over his chest. Lisa then sat on the edge of the bed with Buddy and helped him tape-record a farewell to Rosemarie that began, "Dear Mom . . . You know you are the last person I would ever intentionally want to hurt on this earth. I love you so much. . . ." As Buddy spoke, Jimmy stepped inside the bathroom. Unable to bear the ordeal of this day any longer, Jimmy turned on the water and let himself disappear into the sound of it. He then splashed some on his face.

Jimmy emerged from the bathroom and again peeked through the drapes. A car passed his window and headed out of the parking lot. The chilly March sun had dissolved into golden hues. Jimmy looked at Buddy on the bed and could see that his bottom lip was quivering. But instead of searching for an extra blanket for him, Jimmy spread himself on top of Buddy, the brother for whom he would have given his own life just to see him get up and walk again. Buddy . . . how Jimmy had prayed for him, what lengths he had gone to just get him to smile.

Jimmy pressed down on him, his big shoulders and chest shielding Buddy from the cold. No words passed between them. Jimmy remembers, "What was there to say? There was nothing to say." But Jimmy could not help but let the years pass over him. . . . *See how he dips his head? . . . Orange! Stand on your head. . . . Jeez, Jimmy, what are you doing swimming with the owner? . . . Thanks, Mom, for getting jam. . . . You're Jim Miley. . . . Are you ready? . . .* For close to half an hour, there was just the sound of their breathing.

There came a knock at the door.

Jimmy looked Buddy in the eyes, leaned down, and kissed him on the lips.

Walls
of
Time

. . . . .

Jimmy, 2011.
CREDIT: MARY OLIVIA KRAM

. . . . .

TWENTY

Moving On

Fourteen years later, Jimmy wraps his big arms around a television set, jerks it up against his chest, and carries it to the door. Wearing a T-shirt with MILEY MOVERS printed on it and a pair of cutoff jeans, Jimmy had moved Nick Diaconis and his wife, Harriet, into this independent-living facility just a few months before—as he remembers, there had been an ice storm that day. But the elderly couple had required more care than their son and their daughter had anticipated, so Bob and Pamela arranged for their parents to go into a place in Germantown that would afford them a higher level of care. Bob called Jimmy again, and on a gray April day he and helper George LeVay show up once again at Wesley Enhanced Living Upper Moreland in Hatboro.

In the living room of an apartment that looks out on a complex of athletic fields, Nick, eighty-eight, sits on the sofa as his belongings are removed piece by piece—out the door, down the elevator, and out into the rear of a sixteen-foot box van. As Bob and Pamela help their mother pack boxes, Nick looks on in silence, his eyes following

Jimmy and LeVay as they walk by. Years before, Nick had been an aeronautical engineer with the NACA, the forerunner for NASA, and later General Electric, where he worked on the design for the heat shields on spacecraft. In later years, he and Harriet opened up a diner. But advancing age had compromised both their health and quality of life. Nick had been diagnosed with congestive heart failure. Harriet had been plagued by an increasing memory loss. In the sixty-two years of their marriage, Nick had become wholly dependent on Harriet, who, Pamela says, is "no longer able to keep things straight." Medication has been missed, meals have been overlooked.

Jimmy goes into the bedroom and surveys the bags of clothes piled on the bare mattress. LeVay appears in the doorway.

"What do you want me to do?" LeVay asks.

"Start taking this bed apart," Jimmy says, "while I get these clothes out of here."

Business had picked up lately for Jimmy. There had been weeks, especially during the height of the recession, when his phone had stopped ringing. No one called—except for Cooper, but that was just to check in, the way they always did. Bills had started piling up. While Jimmy had finally paid off the $40,000 van a few years before, a whopping $761 per month for five years, he still had considerable overhead. There was gas, liability insurance, and the $13 an hour he paid his day workers. Buddy had given him the house, but Jimmy was still paying it off, in addition to other personal expenses he had. Money seemed to fly out of his hands. But with the arrival of spring, the general anxiety that had come with the shortage of work seemed to subside as calls began coming in. It was not as it had been a few summers before, when he worked ninety straight days without a break. But Jimmy no longer wanted to work that hard, if only to lessen the wear and tear on his body.

With his fiftieth birthday not far off, there are days when Jimmy wakes up and every bone aches. Feet, ankles, knees . . . he comes home at the end of the day and packs them in ice. "Always sore," Jimmy says. "Always, always, always." Some of it is from his car accident, but to a far larger degree it is just the physical beating that he has absorbed on the job. Whenever he walked into an apartment or a house and looked around, he would think of that corner china closet or that antique armoire as his "opponent" that day—something to be subdued. Once, he tripped on some steps and broke a leg. For a year or more, he has had a pinched nerve in his back. Because of exorbitant health-care costs—which soared to $415 a month from $99 in just a few years—he has dropped his insurance and is unable to get the attention that his injury necessitates. The pain is intense. Jimmy says, "Nothing has ever come easy."

But not just the physical aspect of his occupation exacts a toll on him. Running even a small business has been full of headaches. Moving Nick and Harriet Diaconis had gone smoothly enough, albeit with some troublesome parking issues at the point of unloading. They were nice people, even if their situation was sad. Every day or so it seems, he walks into another small drama: Someone is being evicted from his or her apartment or house; someone is leaving her husband or boyfriend while he is at work. Generally, it goes easier when he has reliable help—such as LeVay, who had been unable to find gainful employment as a mason. But lining up workers who are dependable has become increasingly hard. He had to fire one fellow for taking a shower in the apartment where they were working. Jimmy shakes his head and says, "Just got in the shower and was in there for close to a half an hour. Made me look bad."

With the van parked once again in the driveway at the end of the day, Jimmy sits back on his sofa, which he had picked up from somewhere. Splayed at his feet is his golden retriever, Wyatt, who Jimmy says is going blind. The living-room ceiling is splattered with black scuff marks, which Jimmy explains are the consequence of practicing his golf swing in an enclosed space. But it is in keeping with the décor of the room—or lack thereof. Since Lisa vacated years ago, the place has become a shrine to bachelorhood. Clutter sits in piles on the floor. Only the stuff he got from Buddy is arranged with any care: a framed Baltimore Colts jersey signed by Johnny Unitas; a bat autographed on the sweet spot by Barry Bonds; and a Heisman ball that Yvonne gave Buddy to replace the original that had been stolen. Some pictures of Buddy are up on the wall, and the scrapbooks that Bob had compiled with such loving care for Buddy are stored away in boxes in the attic.

Seldom is there a day that Jimmy does not think of Buddy, how it ended that evening in Michigan. There was that knock at the door, and as Lisa remembers, "Everything seemed to speed up." Into the room swept two Kevorkian aides, Janet Good and a man Jimmy could not identify, and then Jack Kevorkian himself, wearing a black hat and dark glasses. Jimmy remembers that Kevorkian, in reference to the *Daily News* article I had written, greeted Buddy by saying, "So, you're the celebrity." As Kevorkian stepped inside the bathroom to assemble the chemicals he would use for Buddy, Jimmy says that the unidentified man leaned over Buddy and secured a tourniquet on his left arm. Jimmy sat on the other bed with Good, who explained to him how the procedure would work. Jimmy looked at Buddy and asked, "Are you all right?" Jimmy says the man then told Buddy, "We don't want to do this if you don't." Buddy looked up at him and said, "I don't want to do it either. I *have* to." Jimmy says the man placed the button that would release the chemicals within reach of Buddy on the bed and then helped Buddy practice dropping his hand on it.

Good gave Jimmy some documents to sign. Jimmy is still not sure what they were, just that he scribbled his signature across the papers and handed them back. Good then asked Jimmy to write a note that would be pinned on Buddy, and he did so: *I'm Albert Miley and I'm from Warminster, PA. I want you to contact my attorney Geoffrey Fieger.* Jimmy handed it back to Good, then looked over at Lisa in the corner and asked, "Are you all right?" Then Kevorkian emerged from the bathroom with his invention, the Thanatron, three glass bottles suspended from a small frame that would be connected to the button on the bed. Jimmy remembers, "Everything was going a million miles an hour."

Someone told him he better go, he had a plane that would be leaving soon. Lisa sat on the edge of the bed, looked at Buddy, and asked him if this was still something he wanted to do. Lisa reminded him, "You can change your mind at any time." But Buddy said no, and Lisa could see in his eyes that "he was ready for this. There was no fear." Lisa then asked him to send her "white feathers"—a sign that he was at peace. Jimmy says that he just stood there, not wanting to leave but remembering what Good had told him, *For your own safety, you better go.* . . . As Kevorkian, Good, and the unidentified man stood over the bed, Jimmy shuffled toward the door, unsure of how to say good-bye to Buddy until he just said . . .

"You're the Man."

Buddy craned his head up from his pillow and replied, "No, you're the Man."

Jimmy and Lisa walked down the corridor, out of the hotel, and into the parking lot. They got in their rental car and found the highway that would lead them back to the airport. Silence filled the car. Then Jimmy told Lisa, "We better call home." Lisa dialed the number and handed the phone to Jimmy, who held it up to his ear. His sister Linda picked up. Jimmy told her what had just happened, where they were, and asked . . . is it okay if I come home? Linda urged him to do just that and added, "We're all here waiting for you." Jimmy then dropped the car off, and he and Lisa headed into the terminal. Jimmy grabbed her by the hand and jumped to the front of the line at the ticket counter, announcing, "We've gotta catch our plane." Jimmy remembers how odd it was that no one objected, as if they knew where he had just come from and why he had to get away in such a hurry. "I had the feeling that they *knew*," says Jimmy. "Like, 'Oh, yeah, shit like this happens all the time in Detroit.'" As their plane began to board at the gate, Jimmy found a phone booth and called the Quality Inn. When someone picked up, he said hurriedly, "There is a deceased body in Room 146." Quickly, he hung up. And he and Lisa got on their plane.

What Lisa remembers when they finally got back to Warminster was the front door opening. Bob hugged Jimmy, then each of his sisters did the same: Joanne, Rose, Patti, and Linda. Jimmy encountered none of the anger he had feared. There was only a sense of deep, deep sadness. Quietly, Rosemarie told him, "Buddy should have never done this to you." Bert sat in a chair in the living room, his face set in a deep frown. His eyes red, Jimmy just said, "It was what Buddy wanted." As the Mileys comforted Jimmy and each other, they were also aware that they were facing some unknowns. None of them knew what would come next. Would Jimmy get in trouble? Would the cops show up and lead him off in handcuffs? Suddenly, he had become thrust at the center of what had become a national news story, one that had sharply divided the country into pro- and anti-Kevorkian camps. In a conversation Jimmy had with Fieger the following morning, the attorney had told him to expect "two days of reporters, then it will die down—something else will happen and they will move on to that."

Good had told him to act normal, behave as it were any other day. So Jimmy did just that, even if his sense of what was "normal" had become irrevocably altered. The same feeling that had enveloped him at the airport in Detroit had followed him home: this feeling that somehow people knew what he had done just by looking at him. Wherever he went, he could not escape what appeared to him to be the judgment of strangers. On his answering machine a day or so later, someone who identified himself as a police detective in Michigan said, "Mr. Miley, would you please call us at your earliest convenience." Jimmy put down the phone and sighed. "Oh, shit." From his front window, he looked down the street to the corner of Acorn and Kingsley, and as Fieger had predicted, TV trucks were camped out with reporters doing stand-ups. But the Mileys had no comment.

Someone had accompanied Buddy to Michigan, but none of the accounts that appeared in the local papers and elsewhere identified Jimmy or Lisa. Jimmy did return the call from the detective. But while he never heard from him again, he fully expected to hear from someone in law enforcement, if not now, then one unexpected day when he would part the drapes and see a patrol car outside by the curb. Given that a police spokesman had been quoted as saying the police did not expect to pursue charges against whoever had come to Michigan with Buddy, Jimmy had perhaps been irrational in his fear that he would be arrested. But the fear would take root deep inside him. Other than the few people he had confided in—his family, Lisa, Cooper, and some others—he told no one. In his appointment with Dr. Michals two days after he got back from Michigan, he did not even bring up what had just happened. It would not come up in a session until that June, but then only in passing and in the context that he seemed to be sleeping better.

Only Cooper had a feel for the torment that Jimmy had slid into. Cooper had spoken with him the day after he got back. Jimmy told him, "Oh, Cooper, it was the hardest thing I have ever done in my life." Cooper could see that he was a ball of worry, unsure of what would happen to him. "Jim," his friend told him, "just stay cool." But Jimmy was far from cool. Inside, he simmered with rage until it swelled to such uncontainable fury that he had to strike out. He would see someone park in a handicap spot without a permit and say, pissed off beyond words, "Dude, is something *wrong* with you?" But when he calmed down, Jimmy would become cognizant of the peril from such unchecked behavior: Someone could end up hurt, and he would end up in jail. To vent, Jimmy worked on the heavy bag that hung from a tree limb in his backyard, beating the sides of it with his big fists. Cooper even offered himself as a target, telling Jimmy, "You want to get your frustrations out? Hit me." So Cooper would come over, and Jimmy would pummel him in the arms as this unmovable force stood there in the front yard and took it. It became such a frequent occurrence that the neighbors would look out and think, *There they go again.*

"Not just the front yard but everywhere," says Cooper. "As soon as he would see me, he would tee off on me. He would punch me in the arm. And I would say, 'Come on, is that the hardest you can hit?' He would get in five or six blows, and then I would finally punch him back. People have told me I hit like Mike Tyson. Well, I would hit him and he would go running off. In a way, it was kind of crazy. Usually, we would end up wrestling on the ground and laughing. He just had to get it out of his system."

Cooper chuckles and adds, "Jimmy is my boy."

Jimmy laughs when he is reminded of those skirmishes. "It was either that or get in a bar fight—and who knows where they would have led. I would call up Cooper and say, 'Come over here so I can beat your ass.' And he would."

Years would pass before Jimmy would come out of hiding. In preparation for a story I wanted to do a year after Buddy died, I drove out to Warminster and sat down with all of the family except Jimmy. They said it would have been just too emotional for him. While no one came out and said that Jimmy had flown Buddy to

Michigan, the conversation made it fairly clear that it had indeed been him. The story appeared on the one-year anniversary date, and that would, I suspected, be where the Mileys and I would part. But I would occasionally speak with Rosemarie, just to say hi, and I would always end the conversation by saying, "Say hi to Jim." I told her I would love to speak with him, but I got the impression from her that I had a better chance of lining up an impromptu lunch with Clint Eastwood. Jimmy had walled himself off in some private hell, not sure what he would find if he ever ventured out.

It was not until eight years later—in January 2006—that Rosemarie called me and said, "Jimmy is ready to see you."

We agreed to have a no-strings-attached talk. At the end of it, if he still did not choose to go forward with a story, I would walk away from it without a word. With the ground rules set, we sat down in a diner around the corner from his house. For four hours, he told me his story, how he had no other choice but to help Buddy. He would do it again, he said, even if some people would look at him and think he had committed some crime. But they did not know Buddy, he said—or the pain he was in. As Jimmy spoke, I could see how he had become a prisoner of what had happened, as paralyzed by his circumstances as surely as Buddy had been by the tragedy that had befallen him. Seeing what had happened the year before to Terri Schiavo had spooked Jimmy. The young woman from suburban Philadelphia had spent years in a vegetative state as her husband, Michael, and her parents, Robert and Mary Schindler, quarreled in the courts over whether her feeding tube should be removed. The political climate was such that Jimmy said at one point during our conversation, "Maybe you should just let sleeping dogs lie." Two weeks later he called to say that he'd decided not to cooperate with the story, only to inexplicably change course and agree that spring.

"People used to ask me, 'How is Buddy doing?'" Jimmy says.

"And I used to ask him, 'What am I supposed to say?' For years he just told me, 'Say I'm doing good.' And I always did that. So when people asked me, I would say that because he told me to—'He's doing good.' As I said it, I was always thinking, *How do you think he's doing? He broke his neck. It sucks, man!* But as the years passed, you could see the hope leave him. And when that goes, you have nothing else."

Jimmy shrugs. "Eventually, it was no longer a question of how he was going to live, but how he was going to die. What were his choices? Go to a nursing home and die there? With bedsores? And with no one there to help him scratch? God, can you believe what an awful death that would have been for him? He did not deserve that. He had an awful life. You know, Buddy was somebody who never got what he wanted. I just thought for once in his life that should happen, even if it was just to die the way he wanted."

Word has circulated back to Jimmy that other people would have taken Buddy to Michigan. Hearing this compels Jimmy to reply sharply, "Like who? Name him!" But there was no one else, or anyone that Jimmy had ever heard of. He has come to think their lives had unfolded by a design, that perhaps he had been spared in his car accident just so he could help Buddy, as Jimmy says, "to get out of Dodge." Perhaps that had been the miracle he had "stolen" from Buddy at Lourdes. But whatever destiny had linked them, Jimmy cannot help but think of Buddy as free now, not unlike the lion in that fable that Lisa had once asked him to read. On the ground lie the ropes Jimmy had gnawed through.

. . . . .

Karen, 2011.
CREDIT: KAREN KOLLMEYER ARCHIVE

. . . . .

TWENTY-ONE

Coveted Time

Ordinarily, Karen would have spent the morning in her pajamas, as she always did on her days off. But on this sunny December day in 2009, she has an appointment at the Wynfrey Hotel, so she dresses in a red jacket and jeans, powders her face, and fixes her hair in a ponytail. She has been separated for more than a year from Ron, but is not alone in the well-appointed house that looks out on Mallard Lake. Her son, Cory, and his baby boy had been living with her for some time, and her daughter, Jessica, and her two sons had recently moved out on their own. Child care has become an unexpected obligation for Karen at age fifty-three. Yet she loves her grandsons dearly and dotes on them, even when they keep her as busy as the job she holds as a registered nurse in the emergency room at a Birmingham hospital.

On the short drive over to the hotel, Karen begins thinking again of Buddy, not sure what she will remember. Shoot, it had been so long ago—twelve years! No longer does she think of him daily, or even weekly, but on certain evenings she stands on her porch and looks up at the starry sky, and she thinks of him up there playing in the Milky Way. She still holds the "unrealized dream" they shared in her heart. In the years that have passed since his suicide, she has spoken to no one of Buddy, not Ron or her now-grown children or any of her friends. It is not that she has secrets to keep, but just that the story would take forever to tell, and even then she wonders if anyone would fully understand.

She does not look like the one picture I have seen of her, snapped at the wedding reception she and Buddy had attended when she was perhaps fifteen or twenty pounds heavier, her face somewhat fuller beneath the French twist she wore that evening. "Oh, that French twist!" she says. "Buddy wanted me in that. I'd never had one before and I've never had one since." As she walks across the hotel lobby toward me, her athletic carriage speaks to a healthy diet and regular exercise that includes daily runs through her neighborhood. Gone is the grinding stress that she had been under when that picture was taken. From the day the private investigator had contacted her until the very end, she had become progressively more on edge. In some place deep down, she knew that she had the power to stop Buddy by just saying the word. But she knew why she had not said it, and the knowledge of that would occupy a place in her conscience for years.

We slide across from each other into a booth at the hotel restaurant and order coffee. Over some small talk, I am struck by her voice, the tender quality it seems to possess. Buddy had loved it—had indeed gone to extravagant lengths to preserve it so he could play it over and over. Karen only became acquainted with that tape later, when it came bobbing to the surface as if it were a piece of seat cushion from some small plane that had crashed offshore years before. But that Buddy had not captured her voice seemed somehow in keeping with the place she held in his life, how as the years unfolded she had become a chimera: here and then gone. Their relationship had been held by Buddy with such privacy that it astonished her that I had even found her.

"Well," I tell her, "he called you just before he died."

"Uh-huh," she says.

"And you were supposed to have your first date with him the day he got injured?"

"Sort of. We were supposed to go out with a group of people."

"Well then?

She smiles. "I knew Buddy . . . Well . . . differently."

When she sat down and added it up, they had spent only a handful of days together once they graduated from high school: that initial visit at the end of 1974, a total of three weeks in 1983, and then sixteen or so days in 1996. In the twenty-three and a half years since she left Buddy behind after high school, they were together no more than forty days. Of course, there were periods when they talked intensely on the phone. But given the relatively few personal encounters between them, the Mileys were understandably puzzled when I told some of them that I had found Karen in Alabama and flown down to interview her. "Karen?" one or two of them said. "Why Karen?" They said it with genuine curiosity, yet upon reflection agreed that Buddy had indeed had a deep affection for her. By and large, they remembered her as "a nice girl." Only Joanne expressed uncertainty concerning her, in part due to how depressed Buddy would get when she left. "I was wary of her because of that," says Joanne. "But perhaps that was just because I was his big sister." Jimmy had few recollections of Karen, other than that she had taken him to a handful of ball games when he was a boy. But Jimmy says, "Buddy seemed to like her, so I liked her." Karen remembers that Buddy wanted to keep her to himself, a desire that had for years perplexed her but one that she came to understand. Karen says, "The time we did have together was coveted. By both of us."

She says, "We used to laugh at how different we were. The hippie chick and the jock. We used to say, 'Nobody will ever understand what we see in each other.'"

Even she seemed not always sure of what the attraction had been, why it had endured for so long under such unusual circumstances. Some of it surely had to do with the attachment that had formed between them so early in their lives. Given her upbringing in a navy family, which had required her to move from place to place and had never allowed her to form deep friendships, Karen had befriended Buddy in a way that was uncommon for her. Had it been a typical high school relationship, chances are they would have dated briefly and gone on with their lives. But this was far from a typical high school relationship. When Karen visited Buddy at the hospital, Karen says, "We spent far more time together than kids usually do. I was there every day for hours. And we spent most of those hours just talking . . . about everything." Karen wonders what would indeed have happened if Buddy had not been injured, if they had become acquainted under ordinary circumstances. Or what would have happened if Buddy had become well again, found her, and swept her off her feet. Karen smiles and says, "Maybe we would have dated for a month and broken up." But, as she adds, the relationship had nowhere to go in the real world, "so it remained in a suspended state." Karen says, "What you should know is Buddy loved so deeply. He was a dreamer."

Given how hard it always was to leave him, that she had missed her plane back to Birmingham on her final visit was not surprising. It was as if the governor had handed down an eleventh-hour reprieve. They had said their good-byes, but now they had to get in the car, go back to Warminster, and do it over again the following day. Buddy told her as they drove, "I can't do this again. Tomorrow, I'll stay home." Understandably, Rosemarie was shocked to see them again as they came through the door, saying as she eyed Karen, "What the heck are you doing here?" When Karen called Ron to alert him not to pick her up at the airport, he said with a sigh, "How could you miss your plane?" But she and Buddy enjoyed that final evening, indeed looked upon it as an unexpected blessing. The following morning, she dressed and gathered her bags, and as Buddy looked up at her from his bed, Karen leaned over and gently kissed him on the lips. Buddy did not say good-bye—he could never bring himself to do that. Instead, he watched her as she walked out the door and peered out his window to the driveway, where she slid into the passenger seat of the car that would take her to the airport. Karen says, "It was awful. It was just . . . ahhh."

She remembers that Ron was cool toward her when he picked her up. She knew that he had not wanted her to take the trip, and now she was a day late getting back. Ron says he "probably was," and that when Karen got off the plane, she was not wearing her wedding ring. Sharply he asked her, "What's that about? You don't wear your wedding ring around him?" Karen told him she always wore her wedding ring, and that she had probably just packed it in her bag without thinking. Still defensive about this in our interviews, Karen points out that she is wearing her ring in the pictures from the wedding reception, and she regrets that Ron has carried this question for so long. They drove from the airport in silence and, once home, split off into their own spaces. Ron was busy with work, always out on sales calls, and Karen had her hands full with their children. It was not something they argued about, or discussed, or even acknowledged again. Nor did Karen bring up the palpable tension that had settled over her house in her continued conversations with Buddy, who called her in varying moods two or three evenings a week. On some days he was up, on others he slipped into depression. Karen became exhausted from the tension.

Given the frequency of his calls over such a long period, it shocked her when Buddy finally told her in March 1997 that he had a firm date with Kevorkian. "It was a short time before, not even a week if I remember," Karen says. Suddenly, it had become real to her in a way that it had not been up until then. Privately, she began having a conversation with herself: *You can stop this. All you have to do is say, "Buddy, come on down."* But she could not bring herself to say it. What if he said yes? How could she do the impossible? As they spoke the evening before he left for Michigan, she continued to be swept up in a whirlwind of confusion, not sure if she could or should stop the events that had been so long in the planning. Overnight, she tossed and turned in her sleep, getting up at 5:00 A.M. as she heard what sounded like Buddy whisper in her ear, *Karen. Wake up.* Having taken off work for a few days that week, she fell back asleep, only to rise an hour later to get Jessica and Cory off to school. As Ron slept, Karen prepared coffee and looked as her children began squabbling over a Cap'n Crunch box, which had a puzzle on the back that both of them wanted to solve.

"Hey, nerd!" Jessica said. "Give me the box. Mom, tell Cory to give me the box."

"Jessica's a butt munch, Mom," Cory said. "It's my turn. I got it last and I'm lookin' at it now."

"Yeah, I know. And you're the last one to touch the milk, too. So you can put it away."

"Shut up, butt munch."

"Don't tell me to shut up, Cory. Try and make me."

By 7:05 A.M., they were out the door. Karen could hear Ron in the shower. She looked down and saw that her hands were shaking. A part of her had wanted to be in Michigan with Buddy to comfort him, just as she had sat by the bedside of dying cardiac patients through the years, their hands folded in hers. But this was Buddy, and going to

Michigan would have been beyond her, perhaps taking some piece of her with him that could never be regained. Ron, aware of what would be happening that day, opened the basement door and, as he was leaving, called out to her, "I'll see you tonight." Then he was gone, without another word. She was overcome with a deep sorrow over what she had done to him, how she had allowed her loyalty to Buddy to come between them. She told herself that it would soon be over and Ron would still be there. They would have time to fix whatever had been broken.

Outside, Mallard Lake shimmered beneath a sunny March sky. Karen remembers thinking, *It'll be spring in three more days.* Alone now in the house, she began pacing up and down, not sure what to do with her hands. It occurred to her that, for all the talking she and Buddy had done, she knew few of the specifics concerning the trip to Michigan, other than that Jimmy would be taking him and they were supposed to go to a hotel somewhere in Michigan. Karen eyed the clock on the wall: nine thirty—or ten thirty in Warminster. The conversation she and Buddy had had the evening before had left her unsettled, so she picked up the phone to call him. No one answered. In the grip of building anxiety, she said aloud, as if she had ventured upon some sudden discovery, "I know nothing about life!" As the day passed, ever so slowly, she continued to pace, not able to sit down or even look out the window at the budding trees reflected off the water. The sun edged lower in the horizon.

Then the phone rang.

Karen picked it up and said, "Buddy?"

"It's me, Karen," he said, his voice cracking. "I'm in Michigan. I'm at the hotel."

"Are you sure about this, Buddy? Do you want to go home?"

"No, Karen. I didn't change my mind. Nothing could change my mind. It would be one hundred times worse for me if I lived through today. I couldn't take that. I just need to tell you I'm sorry. I'm sorry, Karen. Remember, after today I'll be free of this broken body."

"Buddy . . ."

"I don't want to leave you. It's unbearable, but not enough to keep me here anymore."

Karen sat down on her kitchen floor. Tears slid down her cheeks. "I'm so sorry. I'm sorry, Buddy."

"I don't want to hurt anyone with this. I never wanted to hurt you. Just know I'll be your guardian angel and take care of you from heaven. Remember, you'll never be alone. I'll always take care of you. You'll be with me when I take my last breath. I love you."

Then he had to go, and suddenly the full emotional weight of what would soon occur so far away crashed down upon her: *Buddy was going to die.* As she sat on the floor, she buried her face in her hands and sobbed, her anguish born of a helplessness that had always been there and had now come over her with choking anger. Outside, the day began to darken as the sky grew heavy with thunderheads. Irrationally she thought, *I have to get on a plane and get up there.* Instead, she went outside and began walking. Lightning flashed overhead as a soaking rain began to fall, gathering in small pools beneath her feet as she splashed through them and told herself, *He is dead now. He has to be.* At some point, she turned to go home, where she began digging up the hard clay under her back deck. As her shovel slammed into the earth, she wondered if this was how it felt to go crazy. Spent, she set down the shovel and went inside, where she showered and changed. Jessica and Cory wandered home from school, and Ron came in later from work. He approached her and asked, "Are you okay?" With her face swollen from crying, she only said, "Yep," and turned away. The subject did not come up between them again.

Karen did not attend the funeral a few days later in Warminster. It was not something Buddy had wanted her to do. But even if he had not told her that, she did not know how she could have looked Rosemarie in the eye given that she had helped Buddy plan his death. Only years later would she understand that, while Buddy had told her she was the only one who knew, he had shared his intentions with quite a few other people. To her surprise, Karen received a call from Rosemarie, who told her that Buddy had died, but not how. Karen expressed her sorrow, but did not let on that she knew of Buddy's plan. A day or so later, Karen spoke to Jimmy, who told her sadly, yeah, Buddy had gone ahead and done it. A package then showed up at her house from Buddy—in it a card, a teddy bear, and a gold charm—and then another came from Jimmy. That one contained an Eagles jersey that Buddy had wanted her to have, and a handwritten note from Jimmy that said, *Call me any time for mourning purposes.* She spoke again a few months later with Rosemarie, who called her just to see how she was doing. Rosemarie told her that Buddy had left a recorded farewell, but that she was not sure she could bring herself to listen to it.

Grief flooded through Karen during this period, yet she had no outlet for it. She did not unburden herself to Ron, who supposed that now that Buddy was gone, some degree of normalcy would settle back into their lives. But Karen began to withdraw and slid into a staggering depression so severe that she curled up on the bedroom floor in a fetal position and wanted to stay there. Days would go by and she would not eat or wash. In the journal where she would jot down her recollections, she wrote, *The urge to lie here is overwhelming and I have to give into it, any desire to move I may have had, expired some time ago. . . . The "off switch" is in my reach. I see it.* Karen says she had no inclination toward suicide, only an urge to isolate herself from the world. Buddy was only referred to in this part of her journal in passing and Ron only in the abstract. Unsure of what to do or say, Ron eventually, asked her, "When are you going to get up?" Karen replied, "Soon," yet in her journal she said that she wanted to yell that her *soul was in pain and splitting in two*. Ron says, "It was pretty frightening."

Stress continued to tear at the marriage even as Karen began to emerge from her depression. Distance had grown between them. Somehow they just stopped talking. Ron moved out in July 1998 with the intention of filing for divorce, yet they reconciled by the end of the year. But Jessica, eighteen and unwed, became pregnant with the twins, Alex and Jax, early the following year. To help out her daughter, Karen says that she became "a new mother again." Whatever plans she and Ron had, either individually or separately, were placed on hold as there were more children to care for. They once again became immersed in separate worlds, with Ron working long hours at his job and Karen helping her young daughter cope with the demands of motherhood. But the pressure on their relationship increased when, as Jessica moved out with the boys, Cory ended his brief marriage and came home with his baby son, Jayden. With tension in the house at a pitch, Karen and Ron separated again and remained apart for three years. Ron moved back in again in early 2011. While both say that the issues that came between them have been deeply layered and extended beyond Buddy, Ron cannot help but feel that Karen had for years remained obsessed with how it had ended for the boy upon whose pillow she had so long ago left butterfly kisses.

Ultimately, what would prey upon Karen was the power that Buddy had given her. Even as troubled as the years have been, she looks back on her life and says she has been surrounded by love. Whatever problems she has encountered have been the stuff of living, the hard edges that can dig into you when you share a life with someone. She had tried to explain this to Buddy so long ago—that this part of life was real—yet she had existed for him in idealized form, a vision he could summon to soothe him in his darkest hours.

Unbidden by her, he had given her immense authority, and she could not help but think that she still held it as she sat on her kitchen floor while Buddy said good-bye to her on the phone. Whether it is true or not, she believes that she could have stopped Buddy had she asked him even then to come to Birmingham. But she could not bring herself to do it. She just wanted it to be over, not only for Buddy but also for her. There had to be an end to this suffering. And it is this inescapable realization that causes her to peer into her soul at certain moments and think, *I killed him.*

Bert and Rosemarie at their fiftieth wedding anniversary, 1997.

. . . . .

TWENTY-TWO

Bagpipes

Softly, an old song from the 1940s plays on the radio in the kitchen, the Vaughn Monroe standard "Racing with the Moon." As Rosemarie sets the table for lunch, a plate of sliced deli turkey, rye bread, and cupcakes, words that she had come to know on faraway evenings during her youth wash over her: *In the blue heavens I see . . . Your face smiling at me . . . My heart will never be free . . . Until we're back together.* It reminds her of those nights at the Benedict Club, when she was so young and unencumbered, drawn by the hand onto the dance floor by a soldier or a sailor who would any day be leaving for battles in Europe or the Pacific. She would remember every one of their faces, and every one of the songs they danced to, yet she slaps me on the arm in private and admonishes me playfully, "Don't ask me questions about them in front of Bert!" Four servicemen proposed to Rosemarie in the first four months that she went to the club. But none of them would settle into her heart the way her husband had.

Where had the years gone? It had been sixty-nine years since they'd met at Exide Battery and Bert headed to the Pacific. In the living room of their small house on Acorn Drive, a place that was once so full with the commotion of children, Bert sits on the sofa, his walker in front of him. As always, he greets me with civility, an off-hand comment or two on how the Phillies have been playing, then slips into a pool of silence. Getting him to talk has always been a challenge, Rosemarie says, and even when he does, he will never open up and let you know what he is thinking. Typically, he will growl, give a terse opinion, or reply with only a dismissive shrug, as he does when I ask if he enjoys Frank Sinatra. "No," he says. "I used to. But enough is enough." Yet in one period in his life, so long ago now, he expressed himself with an eloquence that would have shocked any-one who came to know him later, surely his alienated son, Buddy. Rosemarie always knew Bert had a sweet sensitivity, even if it only still existed in the frayed letters she kept in the drawer by her bed that no one but her ever saw. For Rosemarie, they would forever be sacred, and she had withheld them from me for better than a year until, quite by surprise, she takes out one of the last letters Bert had written from Tinian before he shipped stateside.

Rosemarie slips the four-page, handwritten letter from what re-mains of the envelope and says, "The date is October 1, 1945."

She begins reading from the final page:

"'Honey, do you realize that as each day passes by that I grow more and more fond of you? Being away from you is like being in hell. I miss you that much. I hope you miss me as much as I do you daily. And if you do you can understand how I feel. It's really awful yearning for someone as much as I do for you sweetheart, but I kind of like it myself. Being in love is a wonderful thing. I'm just dream-ing of the day I get back so I can take right up from where we left it off in May. We were the happiest couple in the world then and I hope and pray that you want the same happiness on my return as much as

I do. You're wonderful honey, the most wonderful thing that ever happened to me . . .' " /

Rosemarie folds the letter back into the envelope and says, "That was the man I fell in love with."

What happened . . . where had that essential piece of him gone? How could someone who expressed himself so openly and with such ardor have become so withdrawn? Rosemarie has pondered that question through the years. Some of it had to do with crowding seven children into that small house, where there would be no privacy and offhand comments were always within earshot. With the arrival of each child he seemed to bend under ever greater financial pressure. But even he would have to concede in his later years, what else does a man strive for in life if not to be surrounded by his children and their children? Notwithstanding his entrenched reticence, he can look at the walls of his house and see the success he has had a hand in, beaming down from wedding pictures. In them are his four attractive daughters, his three fine sons, two upstanding sons-in-law, and the blessed grandchildren that Bert can be spotted cooing over in old family movies. But Bert can be that way, an on/off spigot that for years has only sporadically dripped with the warmth that Rosemarie knows that he keeps inside.

On the wall in the bedroom hallway is another picture, of Buddy, shot just a few weeks before his death. Whenever I visit with the Mileys, I pause over it: Buddy does not appear to have a care in the world. Spread across his face is an easy grin, and the full beard he always wore during the winter. Rosemarie always scoffed at the vegetation on his chin with a sparkle in her eye. "Oh, Buddy, that beard has got to go!" Unwittingly she added, "If you still have it when you die, I'm going to get the undertaker to scrape it off!" Nothing in the picture gives a clue or foreshadows in any way the events that would soon unfold. When Rosemarie searches her memory of those last few weeks, she saw nothing that would indicate that Buddy was on the verge of taking his life. On the day that he died, she had no inkling that anything was amiss until early evening, when Bert looked out the window and called to her in the kitchen, "Our girls are outside. Why are they here?"

The sun had just set that cold March day as daughters Rose, Joanne, Patti, and Linda climbed out of a car and walked up the driveway. When Linda had heard from Buddy in Michigan, she immediately contacted her sisters, just as they had planned at the meeting at her house a few weeks before. The plan had been for them to drive to Linda's house, then the four of them would deliver the news in person to their parents. On the trip there, they discussed who would do the talking. Joanne and Patti said they could not do it, so Rose volunteered to take charge. Inside, their brother Bob was in the basement working with weights when he heard Rose call to him. "Give me a second," he replied. But Rose snapped, "Get up here now!" Alarmed, their parents sat down in the living room, Bert on the sofa and Rosemarie in a chair.

"What happened? Did something happen to Buddy?"

"Mom," Rose began, "Buddy went out to see Dr. Kevorkian."

Rosemarie gasped. The first thing she could think of to say was "He made Jimmy do that?"

Bert rubbed his head and said sorrowfully, "Oh, boy."

Bob emerged from the basement door. Linda intercepted him and said, "Your brother's not coming home."

Confused, Bob replied, "You're crazy. He lives here."

"You're not listening. Your brother's not coming home," Linda repeated.

As he glanced at the solemn faces surrounding him, it dawned on Bob what she was saying. Buddy had asked him in December if he had any thoughts around suicide, and Bob replied with vehemence that he was against it. "Don't give it another thought," Bob told him. Buddy just changed the subject. It was the first inkling Bob had had of what Buddy was thinking of doing. Bob says, "I was shaking, I was so angry." He would come to change his position as he conceded that he had been thinking more of himself than of Buddy. Bob enjoyed stopping in to see Buddy at the end of the day, had looked forward to how they would sit and talk. Bob had come to the house that March day to do precisely that, yet as he steered into the driveway prior to the arrival of his sisters, he was overcome with "an eerie feeling that something was wrong." The van was always in the driveway. It was gone. Inside, he checked the "green box" on the shelf where Buddy used to keep some petty cash for incidentals. Oddly, only some loose change was in it. But he had no immediate suspicion of what Buddy had done, and it stunned him when he heard that his brother had gone to Kevorkian. "Holy mackerel!" Bob said. "How did he get in touch with Dr. Kevorkian?" Unable to grasp what he had just been told, Bob hurried from the house and went over to see a fellow teacher, Bob Kennedy. "I could see as he came up the driveway that something was wrong," says Kennedy. "Bob just said, 'Buddy is dead.'"

Somber acceptance settled over the Miley house. Uncle Bob and his wife, Aunt Eileen, came down, followed soon by other family members. Two Catholic priests were summoned. Occasionally, Rosemarie wondered aloud, "Do you know if he's dead yet?" Bob came back and sat in the backyard with neighbor George Bushman. In the endless hours that passed as everyone waited for Jimmy to get back, a few calls were placed to let some close friends know what had happened. One went out to Dave Heilbrun, the United Airlines pilot who years before had built the addition for Buddy. Told by Buddy that he had an appointment with Kevorkian, Heilbrun had been flying that day over Detroit and looked down from his cockpit window.

He remembered, *Buddy is down there today.* A tear dripped from his eye. Neighbor Sue Schultz received a late call from Bob, who left a message on her answering machine that said, "Mrs. Schultz, I saw your light on. I just wanted to let you know Buddy died." It was late— she told herself she would go down the following morning—but as she pondered what had happened, she remembered how Bert and Rosemarie were the first to come by her house when her eighteen-year-old son, David, died in a diving accident on Easter Sunday in 1977.

Seeing Jimmy show up was a relief to Rosemarie. When he and Lisa parked the van, their long day now over, she could feel some of the tension ebb from her frail body. Bob went outside and embraced Jimmy in a hug. With tears in his eyes, Jimmy then stepped back, looked at Lisa, and told his brother, "Hug her." Once inside, Jimmy hugged everyone, then turned to his mother, whom he swallowed up in his large arms. As Jimmy heaved with grief, she wondered how he would handle this, not just then but in the years to come. But as she leaned against her boy, Rosemarie would not let herself cry, not then or later that week at the funeral or the cemetery. Whenever she had the urge to, she remembered what Buddy had always told her: "Mom, when I die, I don't want you crying for me." She remembered how he would describe the tunnel of light he walked into when he was injured so long ago, and what he had told her: "If you ever saw that tunnel of light, you would never be afraid to die."

With the note Jimmy had written pinned to his chest, Buddy was found the following day at 9:00 A.M. when his sister Rose called the Quality Inn to report a death in Room 146. Apparently, no one had acted on the call from Jimmy the previous evening from the airport. Jimmy says, "I had been in such a hurry the person who answered the phone probably thought it was a crank call." Because it had the earmarks of a Kevorkian case, there was a brief police investigation, which delayed the release of the body pending an autopsy. But Wayne County prosecutor John O'Hair would not press charges, which had been his stated position in assisted suicides. Geoffrey Fieger, an attorney for Kevorkian, told the Associated Press that Buddy was "a very bright and courageous man who couldn't put up with the pain. . . . He said he didn't want to exist like that for one minute longer." Fieger declined to be interviewed for this book.

Cars came and went from the house on Acorn Drive in the days that followed, some bearing old friends who were allowed entrance, while reporters were politely asked to leave. Inside, Buddy's room was cleaned out by his siblings, who arranged for his hospital bed to be removed and packed up his belongings in boxes. In the closet, they found a bottle of Southern Comfort and each poured down a shot in honor of Buddy. Later, they sat out back under the stars, and Patti and her husband, Rudy, looked up at the moon and swore they could see Buddy in it. Everyone else looked, but only those two could see it. There it is, they exclaimed—his face! He even has a beard! Buddy still had his beard when he died, but Rosemarie did not follow through with her promise and order the undertaker to scrape it off. At the funeral home, Patti spotted a brush that had been left by his casket and worked on his hair one final time. When she was done, it was perfect, just as he had always liked it.

Five hundred people crammed into St. Joseph's Church for the funeral on March 25. Canon law once specifically barred a Christian burial to a suicide, but Father James A. Grant, the pastor at St. Joseph's, told the *Catholic Standard & Times,* "Our insights into psychology didn't become prevalent until the 1940s. . . . I haven't seen a case where Christian burial was denied to a person who committed suicide in the past 30 years. The only thing we can do is pray, and in our prayer, hand Buddy over to God." Nine priests sat on the altar. Old coaches, teammates, and neighbors poured into the pews, along with current students and players from Archbishop Wood and William Tennent. Coach Juzwiak consoled Jimmy, who stood uneasily amid the crowd in a $500 suit that his sister Rose had allowed him to charge to her credit card. The coach had attended mass every morning since Buddy had been injured. Aware of what Jimmy had done, Juzwiak hugged him and said, "You did okay."

Quite a few tears were shed that day for Buddy as Jim Murray gave the eulogy. With his customary sense of humor, the former Eagles general manager lightened the mood somewhat when he called the trip by his old friend to Michigan "the ultimate quarterback sneak." Murray characterized Buddy as "a hero," someone who "spent his whole life living Lent." Murray, who had spoken to Buddy just a few days before his death, added that his friend lived the Passion of Jesus Christ: not only did he carry his own cross, he helped others to carry theirs. At the end of the service, the remains were removed from the church and placed in the hearse, which led a long procession through Warminster to Holy Sepulchre Cemetery. There, bagpipes played as each mourner passed by the casket and placed a red carnation on it. Stoically, Rosemarie lowered her eyes. But Bert held his hand on the side of the casket and kept it there as he sobbed uncontrollably over the son who had slipped away from him years ago and who was now gone forever.

Whatever painful truth Bert came to that day would remain sealed behind his grief. As he sits in his living room with some old scrapbooks at his feet, Bert holds on to a version of history that is devoid of regret. Sure, he says, he saw some of himself in Buddy. They were both fine athletes. "Buddy possibly could have been a pro athlete. I think so," Bert says. He remembers Buddy and a car full of friends beeping the horn as they drove into the driveway one day. Buddy had just pitched a no-hitter in an American Legion game. But Bert could not abide the cocky attitude Buddy projected. He told

Buddy so: "Stop being such a hot dog out there!" Eventually, Bert says, he stopped pressing that and other issues that came up.

"I would let Rosemarie handle it," Bert says. "Because I probably knew he would not pay any attention to me."

I ask him, You believed that?

"I would say, in general, he did not pay any attention to me."

So he tuned you out?

"Yeah."

And you gave up?

"Yeah."

Had he ever communicated to his son any sense of approval?

"Probably not. Probably not."

Had he had any heart-to-heart talks with Buddy?

"No," Bert replies, "Jimmy had the heart-to-heart talks with him."

Outside the dining-room window, a cherry tree that was planted by relatives in commemoration of Buddy stands in full bloom. By the spring of 2011, he would have been fifty-five—in his thirty-eighth year as a quadriplegic. Had he not gone to Kevorkian, Rosemarie believes Buddy would still be alive, yet she concedes that quadriplegics commonly have problems with kidney failure and other issues. Still full of energy at eighty-six, she says she would have cared for Buddy until her final breath. Then Buddy could have moved in with his sister Patti and brother-in-law Rudy. But Rosemarie knows that Buddy would not have wanted to impose on them, that years of depending on others had weighed on him psychologically. "When you are injured the way Buddy was, you are dependent on someone else for your every need," Rosemarie says. "And it is just horrible."

To some extent the hope that Buddy had has come true: Rosemarie has lived a less stressful life since her son died. While it has been impossible to get Bert out of the house, she goes to mass each morning and is active socially with some of the friends she has at the church. Jimmy says, "She has not taken advantage of her freedom as much as Buddy would have liked." Friends say she seems to have far more vitality than she once did, that she no longer appears as exhausted as when she had Buddy under her care. But the years have claimed her dearest friends: Gone are Mary Jane and Betty and Catherine and Rosemary, the girls she used to accompany to the Benedict Club and go out with later for pie. "One day I would like to go to Normandy and see the cemetery there," she says. Over a cup of coffee, she sits down each day to do the crossword puzzle in the *Philadelphia Inquirer*, always calling on assistance from Buddy if she gets stumped. "Come on, Bud!" she'll say. And sure enough, the elusive word will pop into her head.

The passing years have only drawn Buddy closer to Rosemarie. She can feel him with her. With the exception of Kevorkian, for whom she has a continuing aversion just on sheer principle, she has harbored no enmity for anyone who had helped her son carry out his plan. She looks upon them with compassion and a degree of lingering worry. Jimmy seems to have healed since he has come out in the open with his story, yet Rosemarie wonders how deep the scar goes, if he can ever truly get over it. While she has not spoken with Karen for years, it concerns Rosemarie that the young woman she once knew feels some sense of culpability for her part. "Nothing is her fault," Rosemarie says. Nor does Rosemarie blame anyone for not calling her and telling her what Buddy was planning to do. "He had had it," she says. That said, she quickly adds, "But if I had known, I would have never let him out the door."

Weeks and weeks would elapse before Rosemarie could finally listen to the recorded farewell Buddy had left for her. But one day she walked into his old room and sat at the desk. On the wall behind her there was a photograph of Buddy with Karen at the wedding reception—Buddy in his tuxedo, Karen with that French twist. On the shelves still sat autographed baseballs and other pieces of memorabilia. Rosemarie flipped open the recorder and slipped in the tape, the one on the other side of which her son had tried to preserve his conversation with Karen.

She pressed the PLAY button.

"Dear Mom,

"You know you're the last person that I would ever intentionally want to hurt on this earth. I love you so much. It's just that this injury and my life just became too intolerable. I couldn't handle it any longer. Without you, I never would have lasted all these years. You've been my tower of strength. You've always been there for me since day one. I don't know what I would have done without you. No one could have asked for a more loving and more beautiful mother than you are. After spending so much time devoting yourself to me, please take the time for yourself to enjoy, relax, and be able to do the things that you want to do now. As I said to you, I will always be with you. I'm with Nana and Frankie now. . . .

"Again, please, please know that I am fine and that I am happy where I'm at. You be good, and whenever you need anything, please call on me, okay? I'm going to let you go now . . . your guardian angel. Love you, Mom. Bye."

Only then did Rosemarie cry. The tears she had promised not to shed came upon her and fell into the tissue she held to her eyes.

Buddy's farewell card to his mother.

. . . . .

TWENTY-THREE

The Envelope

With one hand on the wheel of his pickup truck, Jimmy looks again at his speech, which he has scribbled on a small piece of paper and slipped inside his wallet. More or less, it is the same speech he has given for ten years or more, changing only a few words here and there and, of course, the name of the recipient who will be receiving the $20,000 college scholarship that Pat Delaney has set up in honor of Buddy Miley. Each spring, the funds are presented to a graduating senior at William Tennent High School who exemplifies the courageous spirit Buddy possessed. On this June evening in 2011, it will be given to Melissa Nunn, who lives around the corner from the Mileys and who a few years ago suffered a diving accident that left her a quadriplegic.

Only sixteen when her accident occurred, Melissa had gone with her family on a vacation to Hawaii. Her parents, Carl and Michelle, had honeymooned there years before, and Carl, a lineman for PECO Energy Company, had saved a small portion from each of his paychecks to go back there for what was planned to be a seventeen-day trip. Five days into their visit, Melissa and her three siblings had gone to swim at Kipu Falls. There, fellow vacationers stood at the top of fifteen-to-twenty-foot cliffs and pushed off through the air into a lagoon below. Excitedly, Melissa went off feetfirst, landed with a splash, and climbed back up to the top to do it again. But as she stood on the edge for her second try, her left foot slipped on some moss as she went off, and she toppled sideways through the air. Unable to extend far enough from the wall of the cliff, she landed head-first on the rocks below. Luckily, an orthopedic surgeon was swimming there that day, as well as two off-duty lifeguards, and she received professional care before she was transported to a hospital. Nonetheless, she had broken her C6 and C7 vertebrae and was rendered a quadriplegic.

As Jimmy approaches the podium in the auditorium, Melissa sits in her wheelchair on the stage with her graduating class, unaware of the award she will be given that evening. She had only gotten a letter saying that she would get one. In the two years that have passed since her injury, she has undergone intense physical therapy, which has enabled her to recover the use of her arms and even her fingers. She has acquired a degree of independence that Buddy never had; she is able to feed herself, push herself along in her chair, and participate in various forms of social networking. While she is no longer able to play softball—which had been a passion for her—she has gone from "an okay student" to a vigilant one. Standing with Sean Delaney, whose parents Pat and Lisa sit in a back row, Jimmy withdraws the piece of paper from his wallet and says:

"The winner this year has unbelievable character and resilience. The student-athlete is Melissa Nunn."

Melissa blinks in surprise.

The crowd erupts in wild applause.

Jimmy leans down and gives her a kiss on the cheek.

The Nunns had known of Buddy for years, yet had not been especially close to him. They knew the story, but not a great deal more. Carl was in the same graduating class with Jimmy at Tennent, but they had known each other only in passing. Michelle had driven by the Miley house occasionally and remembers seeing the hospital bed in the window. Melissa had not been born until 1992 and had never even heard of Buddy until she had been injured herself. But one day Carl and Melissa were invited down by Rosemarie Miley, who gave Melissa a Phillies jacket that had once belonged to Buddy. Given the autonomy of having the use of her arms and hands, Melissa cannot imagine the ordeal that Buddy faced, of having to depend on someone else for his every need. She can fully understand why Buddy had chosen to see Kevorkian.

"I think I can, yeah," says Melissa, seated at her outdoor patio, as Dottie, her springer spaniel, plops at her feet. "I know that I am very lucky to have arm and hand movement, because you can do stuff for yourself. Mentally, I would be in a different place without that ability, so I am not sure I would want to go on living. I think it would be too upsetting. I am amazed Buddy held on as long as he did. I am not sure I could have."

On the day that I visit Melissa, the news breaks that Kevorkian has died at age eighty-three at a Michigan hospital. I ask Melissa her opinion of him. "It was a good thing, if what he was doing was helping people who were in irreversible pain," says Melissa, who has had none of the excruciating pain that afflicted Buddy. Michelle, her mother, adds, "I always applauded Kevorkian for what he did. And I always said, if something were to happen to me, I would want to go with him." But Carl Nunn is not so sure what to think. When he had heard of Kevorkian years ago, he agreed that he was doing a "good thing," that "we do it for animals who are beyond help, so why not humans?" But when Kevorkian appeared on *60 Minutes* and not just assisted but injected Thomas Youk, who suffered from an advanced case of ALS, it seemed to Nunn that Kevorkian had not just crossed a legal line but one of propriety. Nunn says that what should have been "a private moment" became instead a "snuff film." Nunn says he began to wonder, "Is this an ego thing with him or what?"

Rosemarie Miley has only this to say: "Good riddance."

I contacted Kevorkian in October 2010, less than a year before his death. Initially, I was supposed to fly to Michigan to see him. Through his friend and archivist, Ruth Holmes, I had been told he was quite eager to help in any way he could. But as the date of our tentative interview approached, he had an unexpected change of heart. Suddenly, he claimed to have no memory of Buddy, who had become for Kevorkian an indistinguishable face among many. Whatever records Kevorkian had once possessed were long gone, if any had ever existed. Whatever protocols Kevorkian had said he'd followed left behind no discernible trail. In so far as Albert "Buddy" Miley was concerned, there would remain no evidence that Kevorkian had contacted a personal physician or set up a formal psychiatric evaluation for him. All anyone can say is that Jimmy copied his records and sent them along with the January 1993 story I had written, "19 Years of Hell." Unlike quite a few of his other cases, Kevorkian did not videotape Buddy, either beforehand to take a statement from him or during the suicide itself. Some of this could be because Buddy was not a terminal case—and in March 1997 Kevorkian was walking an ever-finer legal line.

With the assistance of Holmes, I set up a telephone interview with Kevorkian in December 2010. As Holmes later informed me, it would be one of the last interviews Kevorkian would do before he fell ill with the kidney and respiratory problems that would later claim him. Convicted of second-degree murder and the delivery of a controlled substance in the death of Youk, Kevorkian had served eight

years of a ten-to-twenty-five-year sentence and had been out of prison
for three years when we spoke for an hour by speakerphone. While
his crusade had made him an international celebrity years before—
indeed, by any account he had become a contemporary icon—his star
power had only increased with the release of the 2010 HBO film *You
Don't Know Jack*. Al Pacino had played him.

But Kevorkian was irritable when he and I talked. In the room
with him were Holmes and his attorney, Mayer Morganroth. Even
though Holmes and Morganroth said that Kevorkian did not remember Buddy, I still hoped that something would come back to him,
something to indicate that Buddy had left some impression and had
not been just another body on what had become a conveyor belt of
assisted suicides. Given how unpredictable his disposition had been,
Holmes counseled me to save any questions about Buddy until later,
but to get started on the topic that had preoccupied Kevorkian since
his prison days: the Ninth Amendment of the U.S. Constitution,
which Kevorkian claimed provides Americans with "latent rights" not
otherwise specifically spelled out in the law. Logically, it would by extension give him cover to have performed assisted suicides; the Ninth
Amendment, however, offered no such leeway to commit murder.

Still consumed by the zealotry that Neal Rubin had encountered
twenty years before, Kevorkian seemed to be energized not by compassion for his fellow man but by the long shadow of some larger foe.
Hand in glove with his scripted set piece on the Ninth Amendment
was an apocalyptic view of humanity, which he predicted would be
steeped in "worldwide slavery within two to three centuries." The
United States, he said, was "a very tight fascist state. . . . We are dealing with a tyrant that you cannot outwit, ever." Overpopulation was
another problem. "We think babies are wonderful, loving. The more
babies, the better. We honor them as heroes or heroines when they
have a baby or when they have eight kids at a time." He characterized

this as "a human tragedy." In light of his opinion that "humans are going to disappear" in the twenty-third or twenty-fourth century, I asked him how he would be remembered, say, one hundred years from now.

"If they [remember] at all, I don't know," he said. "I'll be vilified by that time."

I asked him, "You think so?"

"Oh, sure. The government will make sure I am universally vilified."

Mankind was a mess, he seemed to be saying, strapped into a system of beliefs born of an underdeveloped "ability to think for ourselves." Medicine creates ways to keep people alive beyond their time. "We have too many people already," he said. "If nature dooms you through other deeds, then die." But Kevorkian added, "Humans are weak and they develop these myths they call religion to feel good . . . [that] we are going to sit up there in the clouds on a throne next to God—whoever that is—and we believe that. Some believe it very well. They believe it just like the truth." From there, he got on the subject of the Spartans, who he said were unafraid of death and supremely stoic.

I asked him if he would have looked upon Buddy Miley as "stoic," given his long years of suffering.

Kevorkian said that he did not think so, that the twenty-three and a half years Buddy endured had been only proof that he was "afraid of dying."

With an edge of incredulity I replied, "He was afraid of dying?"

"Otherwise," Kevorkian said, "he would have kicked it after the first year of being paralyzed. . . . After a year of being paralyzed, even if you got something that helped you a little, what good is that? What are you going to do?"

I told him how Buddy had gone to Lourdes and elsewhere in search of a cure.

"He had the hope of being helped," Kevorkian said. "Of course, he could have saved his family twenty years of their suffering. Maybe they did not look like they were suffering. But they were."

So did he have a working definition of a strong human being?

"You take life as it comes. And you do it without crying, without struggling, and without being a burden to anyone else. Might as well take what nature dishes out."

(Holmes later sent me a clarifying e-mail: "The older JK gets, the more bleak his view of life. I always thought it started with so many family members killed in the Armenian Genocide. . . . Prison made him darker still. . . . I would call Buddy very stoic and I would have done exactly what he did. His courage and determination are inspiring.")

Even if his explanation for not remembering Buddy seemed reasonable enough—that no doctor can remember every one of his patients—it troubled me that Kevorkian had forgotten him. Had he been only able to say, "Oh, yeah, the football player," that would have been, well . . . something. But Kevorkian could not even remember that. I wondered if it was just old age or even if he simply looked upon his patients as a means to an end, that none of them existed in his memory in any enduring human form, but as just fodder for the cause that was far larger than any one set of circumstances. Ultimately, I think Buddy should have had a better death, that instead of expiring in a cold hotel room in Michigan under the cloak of secrecy, he should have had someone near who loved him. But he had the only death that was available to him: in the hands of strangers far from home, wrapped up in the saga of an odd man. Arthur Caplan, a University of Pennsylvania bioethicist, wrote this observation about

Kevorkian in a column that appeared in *The Philadelphia Inquirer:*
"Despite his skill in administering potassium chloride to the fearful,
disabled, lonely, and inadequately treated, Kevorkian was a poor
choice to lead the movement to legalize assisted suicide." Caplan
added that the Kevorkian biopic that starred Pacino should have
been entitled *Homicide: Death in a Van at the Hands of a Nut.*

Someone once told Rosemarie that they heard another person call
Buddy a "coward" for how he chose to end his life. "It hurt," Rosemarie says. "Whoever said it had no idea what Buddy went through."
An organization that called itself Not Dead Yet of Central Pennsylvania: People with Disabilities Against Assisted Suicide weighed in
online. In a press release that was published March 21, 1997, Not
Dead Yet wondered, *Was [Miley] killed because he was a quadriplegic, or because he was depressed?* Moreover, NDY asked, *Who pushed
his wheelchair across the room, how did he get into bed, and who tucked
the covers around him?* A letter to the editor in the local *Intelligencer*
also expressed skepticism. *What a terrible tragedy; Buddy Miley was
a man who deserved to live,* wrote Heidi Gerstemeier, of Warminster.
*My belief is that he had a lot to offer. The question remains: Why? Was
it truly pain? We will never know.* But anyone who knew Buddy knew
better than to ask that question.

"Are you shitting me?" Delaney says. "How would you like to
have your balls put in a vise and—every so often—twist! No one has
ever had more resilience than this guy. God! Whenever I would go
see him, he would ask, 'How are you doing?' And I would say, 'How
am *I* doing?' How am *I* doing?' How are *you* doing? How the fuck are
you doing?"

Hearing Kevorkian say that Buddy would have been better off if
he "kicked it after the first year" to save his loved ones the hardship of
caring for him caused me deep consternation. In his inability to see
life—only death—Kevorkian could not begin to understand the light

that Buddy still spreads into the lives of the people who knew him. Were it not for the profound effect that Buddy had on him, Pat Delaney would not have funded a scholarship in his honor, and Melissa Nunn would not have a $20,000 college scholarship, which she can use not just for educational opportunities but also for the technological advances that will allow her to live a fuller life. But on a deeper level, Buddy provided instruction by example to others on how to bear the pain that would come into their lives. Yvonne Ameche Davis . . . whose loss of a son was "something for which there is no compensating." Carmen Frangiosa . . . who found himself thinking of Buddy when his wife was diagnosed with brain cancer in 1998 and died six years later. "She went through hell," he says. And Steve Bernardo . . . who played with Frangiosa at Plymouth Whitemarsh and Wake Forest, who lost his youngest son, Vince, who had an enlarged heart and died running wind sprints on the first day of football practice at Shippensburg University. None of them could explain the randomness of these events, just as Rosemarie had not been able to explain what had happened to Buddy.

Years have passed, and they still miss him. You could see that in the way they spoke of him. Inevitably, tears would well up in the eyes of the people I interviewed, even those who had said given the years that had passed, they could not imagine what they would remember. But they did. His sister Patti told me, "I miss my brother, but not the terrible pain he was in." His other siblings said more or less the same. When I asked some of them how Buddy would be doing if he were still alive, some of them overlooked that he had ever been injured and said, "He would have had his own business, a wife and some children, and probably have done some coaching." It was how they wanted to remember him and would always, as if that split second on the football field at Plymouth Whitemarsh years ago had never occurred.

Occasionally, he comes back to them. Rosemarie is sure that

Buddy helps her with her crossword puzzle, just as Patti and Rudy are sure they once saw his face in the moon. Jimmy says he still feels Buddy around him, that he has prayed to him for help and that those prayers have been answered. Some of it could be coincidence, but Lisa Lepri is certain that it is not. Two weeks before she drove down to Warminster to meet me for an interview, she was standing in her kitchen when a tiny white feather glided down before her eyes. It seemed to come from nowhere, yet it did not surprise her. Gently, it fell in her hand. She placed it in the envelope she had started keeping years before, the one that held the white feathers that she had asked Buddy to send her on that dark night so long ago.

Buddy and Jimmy at Jimmy's tenth birthday party, 1971.

Acknowledgments

Characteristic of her cheerful manner, Rosemarie Miley used to joke occasionally during our many chats, "Oh, brother, I never should have written that letter to *Sports Illustrated!*" Had she not done that—and given me a glimpse into the ordeal her son Buddy endured—chances are I would not have written this book, nor would I have had the honor of meeting her. In reliving events that were so sorrowful, she was unstinting in her patience and kindness. I am deeply thankful to her, as I am to her husband, Bert, and their children: Bob; Joanne; Rosemarie; Linda Farrell and her husband, Mike; and Patti Rudolf and her husband, Rudy. Without exception, they were gracious, candid, and helpful in whatever way they could possibly be.

Certainly, it would not have been possible to do this book without the full cooperation of Jimmy Miley, who overcame his initial trepidation and entrusted his story to me with a courageousness that I found inspiring. In the long hours we spent together over the years, Jimmy was observant, unassuming, and earnest. Abiding love had guided him on his journey to Michigan with Buddy, and it guided him again years later in the preparation of this book.

Karen Kollmeyer aided me in ways that I cannot begin to count. I asked her to help me "tap into the heart" of this story and she did that—and then some. From the beginning, there was no question I asked her that she did not provide a thorough, thoughtful answer, even if the work would prove to be a painful excavation. But she did so always with generosity and intelligence. I would also like to thank her husband, Ron, and their two children, Jessica and Cory; her parents, Bob and Janet Shields; and her siblings, Amrit Khalsa (formerly Linda Shields) and Tom Shields.

Of the many other people I interviewed for this book, I would like to acknowledge a few who were especially helpful: Steve Bernardo; George Bushman; Mark Cooper; Yvonne Ameche-Davis; Mike Dippolito; Bob and Pamela Diaconis; Guy Driesbach; Tim Erlacher; Carmen Frangiosa, Jr.; Grant Hudson; Dave Heilbrun; Bill Juzwiak; Bob Kennedy; Joanne Johnston; Lisa Lepri; Bob Levy; Flos Lutz; Eileen Miley; Florence Miley; Gary LaRocque; Bob McCarney; Jim Murray; Dr. Timothy J. Michals; Dr. Donald L. Nathanson; Steve Nauta; Melissa Nunn and her parents, Carl and Michelle; Neal Rubin; Sue Schultz and her children, Diane and Donnie; Brian Sheehan; Dr. Joseph Torg; and Mary Jane Williams. At Magee Rehabilitation Hospital, I would like to thank Dr. Guy W. Fried and Mary Schmidt.

I am grateful to Ruth Holmes in Michigan for helping me to line up Dr. Jack Kevorkian for what proved to be one of the final interviews he had before his death. Thank you also to attorney Mayer Morganroth and Kevorkian aide Neal Nicol.

I owe a deep debt of gratitude to Pat Delaney for his support and encouragement. Thank you also to his attorney, Brian Price.

Special thanks are due Andrew Blauner, who is not just a fine literary agent but also a fine man. Early on, Andrew shared the vision and passion I had for this project. I am thankful for how he hung with it, and for our friendship.

I could not have been more delighted that we were able to place this book with George Witte, the editor-in-chief at St. Martin's Press. I appreciate the leap of faith he took on me as first-time author, and the care with which he and his staff handled the manuscript.

For their advice and help at points along the way, I would like to thank Steve Carroll; Norman Chad; Frank Deford; Mike Downey; Peter Goldberg; Eliot Kaplan; Chic Kelly; Jackie Koenig; Tom Lachman; Jeanne Leto; Jennifer Rohrer; John Schulian; Peggy Speake; Mindy Tamaccio; Brian Toolan; Erica Vanstone; and Paul Vigna. I would also like to thank my colleagues at *The Philadelphia Daily News:* editor-in-chief, Larry Platt; his predecessor, Michael Days; managing editor, Pat McLoone; and executive sports editor, Josh Barnett. Deputy sports editor, Doug Darroch, was especially helpful in preparation of the copy. At the Newspaper Guild of Greater Philadelphia: president, Dan Gross; executive director, Bill Ross; and attorney, Neal Goldstein.

Finally, I would like to express my gratitude to my family; my mother, Joan, and my late father, Mark, who left me with more than he could ever know; Tracey Franz; Kerry Goldberg; Rene; Alix; Raymond; and Robert. But no one gave more of themselves to this book than my immediate family: my daughters, Cory and Olivia, and—above all—my wife, Anne, who graced each page of this book with her love and wisdom.